Leadership in Action

Leadership in Action

Keys to Ensure School Success

Jim Dueck

ROWMAN & LITTLEFIELD
Lanham • Boulder • New York • London

Published by Rowman & Littlefield
An imprint of The Rowman & Littlefield Publishing Group, Inc.
4501 Forbes Boulevard, Suite 200, Lanham, Maryland 20706
www.rowman.com

6 Tinworth Street, London SE11 5AL

Copyright © 2020 by Jim Dueck

All rights reserved. No part of this book may be reproduced in any form or by any electronic or mechanical means, including information storage and retrieval systems, without written permission from the publisher, except by a reviewer who may quote passages in a review.

British Library Cataloguing in Publication Information Available

Library of Congress Cataloging-in-Publication Data

Names: Dueck, Jim, 1946- author.
Title: Leadership in action : keys to ensure school success / Jim Dueck.
Description: Lanham : Rowman & Littlefield, [2019] | Includes bibliographical references.
Identifiers: LCCN 2019023447 (print) | LCCN 2019023448 (ebook) | ISBN 9781475852370 (cloth) | ISBN 9781475852387 (paperback) | ISBN 9781475852394 (epub)
Subjects: LCSH: Educational leadership. | Educational tests and measurements. | Grading and marking (Students) | Academic achievement.
Classification: LCC LB2806 .D835 2019 (print) | LCC LB2806 (ebook) | DDC 371.2--dc23
LC record available at https://lccn.loc.gov/2019023447
LC ebook record available at https://lccn.loc.gov/2019023448

Contents

Preface	vii
Introduction	ix
1 Who Is the Client?	1
2 Bonding with the Home	5
3 The Truth and Nothing But	13
4 Bonding with Students	23
5 Teacher Supervision and Development	31
6 Grade Level of Achievement	43
7 Teachers' Inconsistency When Assessing Students	47
8 Grade Inflation Is Not Uniformly Evident	75
9 Superintendent Leadership	91
10 Coaches Are Not Reliable Evaluators	103
11 Provincial and State Leadership	117
12 Fully Enlisting Parents	131
13 Using Student Report Cards for Schools	145
Conclusion	155
References	157

Preface

The injunction to leave a situation better than you found it may be an over worn piece of advice, yet school leaders must attempt to do just that with all their rigor and vigor when working within the school system. Effective leadership in our school system identifies key educational perspectives and applies sufficient energy and insight in their implementation. Fulfilling an administrator function in schools, districts, and provincial or state educational services transcends a managerial function when leaders assume risks for ensuring fairness to all students.

This book identifies activities and programs for achieving higher levels of success when working with students, parents, teachers, and school administrators. The medley of proven ideas is not from researching the thoughts and experiences of others but from my personal work. Therefore, research about strategies for school reform from other publications are not incorporated; that said, the concepts I promoted while working in senior levels of leadership do incorporate research, because a body of knowledge was necessary in order for me to validate the leadership activity and advice for which I was advocating.

Placing students atop education's pinnacle requires a commitment to address individual needs and assess achievement fairly and consistently. Considerable progress has been made in our capacity to assess individual student progress, and a proven method for enhancing this assessment is provided in this book. Significant opposition to assessing the system as a whole, fairly and consistently, remains, however, and leadership activities and perspectives for achieving fair opportunity are outlined herein.

The philosophical perspective throughout this book is that education administration is more than mere management; definitively and effectively responding to situations requires effective management. Rather, leaders must use their influence to effect change that leads to improved outcomes. Leaders must constantly be mindful of the data pertaining to these outcomes and strategize to improve them.

The capacity to make decisions, or exercise power, remains a significant concern for numerous players within the education system. Increasing parental involvement in a child's education is a concern, because some parents are involved while too many are not. Charter schools provide one model for relocating the locus of control over a child's education toward the parent, and other less formal arrangements exist and are documented here for the reader's consideration.

Increasing accountability in our education system underpins any effort at educational reform, because school systems spend substantial amounts of tax dollars and so must be held accountable for how they spend. This book documents a comprehensive approach to such a reform, which ensures that the public is well informed about their schools' successes—and failures. When appropriate accountabilities are in place, power transfers from educators to parents, because parents not only have a voice but also the right to make informed choices.

Introduction

This book opens and closes with generalizations pertaining to accountability in education by emphasizing that taxpayers are the school system's clients, while governments' responsibilities include identifying desired outcomes for its citizens and improving these during its term in office. Therefore, government is responsible for devising the education system's accountability framework—a framework based on public consultation that is part of a mutually agreed upon process for evaluating performance within the school system.

The Departments of Education rely on administrative supports to provide leadership for improving outcomes. These administrators work throughout the school systems as school principals, district superintendents, or DOE officials. Therefore, chapters 2 through 12 articulate specific actions and philosophical perspectives that these administrators might find helpful to maintaining and improving educational outcomes.

Readers are assisted by subheadings in chapters that articulate these various strategies for each applicable level of leadership. Each action item outlined specifies its purpose as well as provides details sufficient to undertake the concept at the appropriate level of the school system. Chapters outlining significant philosophical perspectives conclude with end-of-chapter notes.

Chapter One

Who Is the Client?

Our political system is characterized by competing groups seeking to acquire and maintain power. It is not surprising, therefore, that controversies arise and decisions become difficult to make in the public sector in general and in our education system specifically. In many respects, the educational enterprise is a microcosm of society at large: many groups struggle to exercise and retain control atop the power pinnacle. Our difficulty in the education sector revolves around efforts to define who the client is and who represents their interests best. In other words, who should have the most power?

The term *power* has a negative connotation: most people have a kneejerk tendency to either resist power or acquire more of it. A feeling of helplessness arises when those in power determine they are the most qualified to make decisions and then endeavor to limit the influence of others. Power in the public sector is difficult to identify, because services do not have the established bottom line that characterizes the private sector, with its profit-and-loss paradigm.

Educators believe that their frequent interaction with students means they know what is in their students' best interests. Therefore teachers and administrators tend to work together, even though occasionally their interests diverge. Their goal is to work in unison—and occasionally even to work against one another—in an effort to lead as many educational initiatives as possible without interference from politicians, parents, or the public. Educators grow immediately skeptical of any initiative when their expertise is discounted or even disregarded. Essentially, the role of the educator is to assist parents in developing children into the kind of adults parents want them to become.

Teachers' unions represent their members' interests while pursuing influence in and control of our school system. They may not appreciate characterizing their overarching purpose as pursuing "less work for more pay," but this thrust explains class-size reduction, more leave with pay, and more release time to prepare or rest, among other more recent alterations made to the school system. Fundamentally, all unions purpose to pursue their members' influence, but unions operating in the public sector may pursue this drive with less accountability, as here profit and loss are not limitations, since government choose to raise funds through taxation or overspend by increasing government debt.

Parents are also players within the school system and join the struggle for increased power and control. They send their child to school anticipating their child will receive the best education available. While choices involving educational methodologies like direct instruction or discovery learning increasingly emerge for parental consideration, parents are mostly concerned about their right or ability to choose the specific school or program they deem the best fit for their child. Notwithstanding parents' logical desire to influence education, workers in the school system frequently lament the absence of parental interest in a child's development.

Politicians are representatives elected to pursue parents' best interests; however, politicians' focus is splintered among a plethora of agencies; they are not devoted exclusively to education. Politically charged issues confront politicians from all corners of government, and they have limited time available to enact measures that will ensure students achieve at the highest level. While few people dispute that our tomorrow is most influenced by today's schools, few politicians understand the complicated politics at play within the education system. Most disturbingly, they often fail to understand fairness in the educational environment.

The public—specifically *taxpayers*—also must be considered as potential clients of our nation's schools. They pay most of the costs of education. Expecting value for the dollar is the public's right! School boards represent the value bestowed on our education systems, because they have, in many instances, the power to levy taxes and control expenditures. Unlike most government agencies, taxpayers have real opportunity to directly influence educational policy.

However, today a significant difference now prevails compared to back when school boards first exercised taxation powers: Early in our history, and when our economy was agriculturally driven in particular, families were considerably larger than they are today. With as many as ten children in their family—and sometimes many more—parents had a long-term perspective on schooling, because their spread of children might span from grade 1 to grade 12. Today's family of one, two, or three children—so much smaller by comparison—greatly reduces the percentage of parents with school-age children, and those parents who have children in the school system are only involved with the school for a short period of time. Therefore parental commitment to educational excellence lags.

Within the general public are subgroups specifically focused on the quality of graduates leaving our school systems. Universities, colleges, and employers are a student's next step upon earning a diploma. These bodies are so numerous that it is difficult, if not impossible, to identify them as an education system's powerbrokers. Serving students' needs is an educational priority, but achieving these agencies ongoing day-to-day involvement in K–12 issues is impossible, and, therefore, these agencies are considered stakeholders whose input requires a time-consuming activity.

In summary, there is no shortage of groups in society who claim the right to speak to the educational process: teachers, administrators, unions, parents, politicians, and taxpayers all claim, with justification, to be clients of the system. Once a student graduates from high school, a number of groups take great interest, each with its own perspective, and each with its own agenda. Postsecondary institutions and employers are the two sectors in society with the most-frequently profiled opinions about the preschool to secondary system, but not even they, taken in the context of all the other influencers, can be described as powerbrokers in the education system.

Given the cacophony of voices demanding a hearing, it is difficult to identify the primary client of our schools. The historic default position has been to identify the bill payer as the primary client; this would mean taxpayers are our schools' primary client and the body holding the government and school boards, with their taxing authority, accountable for the money they raise and oversee.

Managerial authority, which typically resides within a governmental agency, includes a reporting responsibility to the taxpayer, who has the right to request regular assessments of the outcomes of the programs they are funding. This is where the education system breaks down, however. In fact, it is fair to say that the reporting aspect has often been an unmitigated failure. Typically government bureaucrats release negative information quietly or bury it in a voluminous report that few read. They also distract the public by cherry-picking the results, which are released and celebrated. In the end, transparency is an oft-declared goal but an infrequent reality.

Meanwhile, educational stakeholders such as teacher unions, universities, and parent special-interest groups, among others, focus on issues important to them and attempt to invoke public support for their concern, believing that the squeaky wheel gets the grease. This grease is frequently in the form of additional funding or legislation aimed at addressing a specific concern.

Politicians win elections on promises of accountability, but genuine attempts to be accountable are rare. This leaves taxpayers confused. The reports circulated under the banner of accountability are carefully selected to feature a failure or triumph that serves a political purpose. This happens enough times, and in the end, we are left with a cynical, skeptical public needing to fact-check every detail—something they are disinclined to do.

A new approach to public-sector accountability is now conceivable thanks to the recent explosive development in modern technology we have enjoyed. Information gleaned through satisfaction surveys can be readily acquired using Internet services and instantaneously analyzed by computer programs. Student learning can be measured using standardized testing and even computerized marking. Student identification numbers enable us to track each pupil throughout their educational journey.

With this wealth of resources, accountability in all government services—and most especially importantly in education—is now possible and its outcomes available for public review, including performance evaluations of students, teachers, and education-system leaders (Dueck, 2018). Compiling this information into an annual report card provides a new and stronger form of accountability, because all outcomes are reported and assessed in one release. This is particularly true if the data, compiled and released to the public, is derived from performance criteria negotiated in a consultative process involving the public.

Implementing such a comprehensive approach to accountability is explained further in chapter 13, and the intervening chapters articulate how governmental education administrators—that is, school principals, district superintendents, and Department of Education officials—can improve outcomes. All of the recommended strategies this book provides have proven to be successful in the workplace and are tailored to the various levels of administration. They are also adaptable to local political, social, and cultural contexts that tend to vary from one jurisdiction to another.

Some of these strategies to enhance accountability may prove difficult to implement in various work environments due to certain political or social issues. These strategies predate the universal availability of social media beyond e-mail. Therefore readers may be able to utilize today's proliferation of advancements in communications to enhance related initiatives.

Chapter Two

Bonding with the Home

A student learns best when a close, collaborative, supportive relationship exists between school and home. Educators today frequently lament the absence of parental support for student learning but often fail to reach out to the parents. Fostering a mutual bond may be the objective for both educator and parent, but the school is primarily responsible for the creation and maintenance of this relationship. Benefits from positive interactions between home and school translate into higher levels of student cooperation while generating greater parental response and support when difficulties with the child arise.

PRINCIPAL'S NOTES TO PARENTS

The necessary information to properly assessing a student's academic ability is provided in chapter 6, which offers an in-depth discussion of grade level of achievement. After information regarding a student's achievement, leadership, and behaviors are collected by the principal from teachers or gleaned from personal interactions, the principal can communicate the observations. Foci for comment may come from:

- Participation rates in school activities
- Orderly and compliant behaviors on the playground and in the classroom
- Role modeling behavior for other students including younger children
- Assuming leadership responsibilities, such as monitoring and membership on committees and councils
- Respectful interactions with staff and students
- Attendance and timeliness
- Excellence in learning and completing assignments

- Demonstrations of creativity
- Sportsmanship during games
- And other quantifiable behaviors.

While there are many ways to communicate these assessments, one of the easiest and most effective, especially when the news is good, is for the principal to attach to the student's report card a *handwritten note* of congratulation to the parents. These reporting occasions are one of the most critical in the school year, when parents are most likely to pay specific attention to the school's significant role in assessing their child's development. Informing parents of progress goes beyond an academic focus and encompasses assessment of social, emotional, and physical development as well as personal effort.

A useful technique for principals is attaching a note-sized piece of paper—captioned "A Note from the Principal"—inside the reporting document so that it will not draw attention during classroom distribution of student report cards. These notes were *handwritten*, which subtly but clearly reinforced the message that the personal communication was important enough to warrant the principal's time. Several students from each class received these notes at each reporting period.

Consider how a note might be phrased:

- "I notice that Corey is very helpful to our school by organizing activities for younger students during recess. His leadership makes this free time enjoyable for many and reduces the potential for behavioral problems with many students. Great example of Corey's leadership potential!"
- "Ted's teacher is really pleased with his current attitude about completing homework. Thank you for supporting our requests that he improve in this area. Together we can really support his success."
- "Linda is so consistently respectful in her interactions with other students and adults in the school. It is obvious that she is practicing your values, and we want to commend you for your success in raising such a well-mannered person."
- "Barbara volunteered her artistic talent to improve the appearance of our hallway bulletin boards. Students are really excited about the new look, and teachers are using it as an example to have students explore their own creativity. Thank you for driving her to school on these mornings, because the busing would have had her arriving too late to do this work. We really appreciate your support!"
- "During this past term, Elizabeth really improved her understanding of division and multiplication using three digits. Her teacher had expressed a concern about this problem in the last report card and is aware that you

have devoted hours in extra coaching at home. Your efforts have really paid dividends, and I want to express appreciation for your help."

Parent responses to these brief handwritten notes was always overwhelmingly positive. Many parents came into the school to personally express their appreciation. This relatively minor additional effort accomplished significant gains in bonding the home and school relationship.

In 1984, one school district requested a series of workshops for aspiring school administrators. This strategy for enhancing parental support was subsequently implemented by several aspiring principals. In 2018, while traveling on vacation, I bumped into an administrator from a school district in Calgary and learned that many principals who had first heard about these "principal notes" from people attending the 1984 workshop were continuing the practice even thirty-two years later.

FAMILY FUN NIGHTS

One school district set for itself the goal of making every parent feel so comfortable with school leadership that they would use the principal's first name. Such informality is not readily achieved through request or command but through repeated interactions at a personal level. Therefore at meetings with parents, collectively or individually, school leaders gave both their first and last names. On many occasions, when parents come to the school for formal activities, such as meetings, performances, and ceremonies, personal interactions are more formal and briefer. Less-formal events are better suited for developing relationships, and incorporating *family fun nights* can provide exceptional opportunities for fostering meaningful ties between home and school.

In several of my schools, annually, for each grade—or for several classes within the same grade in larger schools—we invited students to a fun night, with at least one parent or relative as their "ticket" for admission. Teachers of these classes were expected to attend; however, the program was organized and managed by school administration, so the teachers attended as guests. Participants were divided into teams upon arrival, with all family members placed on the same team, and were given an initial assignment to introduce themselves to the parents on the other teams.

Over the years, we developed a number of group activities that provided a sense of accessibility and fun on our family fun nights:

- *Newspaper search:* Each group is given a newspaper with a list of questions answered within the newspaper.

- *Relays:* Groups identify participants for each relay event and earn points for their team in activities involving minimum levels of skill.
- *Find the number:* Numbers are written on one-inch-square pieces of colored paper and then hidden about the school. Participants receive a sheet of clues to each location.
- *Find it:* A chair is place in the middle of the auditorium, surrounded by all teams. Participants are told to find a specific item—like a membership card, a stick of gum, or an eraser, for example—and are to sit on the chair as soon as they have located the item. The first group to have a team member occupy the chair with the identified object wins a point.
- *Wrap-up activity:* To conclude the evening, each group chooses a children's songs from a provided list and is asked to rewrite the lyrics to focus on some aspect of the school. Each team sings their song to the assembly.

Recall that the emphasis of a family fun night is placed on *fun*, for the purpose of building relationships between staff, students, and parents. Each administrator's personal style will determine the best format these activities should take on their own family fun night, but speechifying should be avoided. Applying some ingenuity can result in enjoyable and effective variations to these suggested activities.

ANNUAL GENERAL MEETING

Annual general meetings—or AGMs—are common in the business community, primarily because presenting an overall financial picture at year-end is a requirement. The school's version of an AGM is frequently focused on a "meet-the-teacher" get-together held during the first month of school, when special programming is also featured. Schools may also provide the opportunity for a parent advisory council to annually review and influence the school's education plan for the year's goals and strategies.

Standardized-testing results and the introduction of educational report cards for school and school districts provides another opportunity for a community to review their school's performance. Whereas business is concerned with profitability, a school can demonstrate its concern with outcomes achieved from taxpayer investment. Performance review should be the only focus for the meeting, and it is unwise to only cherry-pick achievements.

An AGM provokes discussion, and school administration should be prepared to channel the session into a productive opportunity for input. The AGM might serve a number of different purposes, such as:

- Introducing parent representatives on the parent advisory council who are willing to provide contact information for ideas, thoughts, and suggestions

- Scheduling some time during the AGM to divide into smaller groups chaired by a parent on the advisory council—discussing things like the school's strengths, weaknesses, opportunities, and threats (SWOT)
- And preparing a form for parents to complete and return to the school, identifying strengths, weaknesses, and suggestions.

Demonstrating transparency and accountability as well as providing opportunity to influence direction are critical aspects of the AGM. A degree of discomfort is inevitable, because some people are naturally inclined to be negative, and so the principal must prepare responses to anticipated concerns.

SELECTION PROCESS FOR A CHILD'S TEACHER

Equalizing teachers' workloads is a thorny issue facing school administrators who are preparing for a new school term. There will be occasions when a specific student should be placed with a specific teacher. When this occurs, plans should be made to compensate the teacher for the workload increase the exceptional circumstances add to their assignment. Simply stated, administrators understand that *not all teachers are equal, and neither are students*. Designing a productive class of students is an important administrative task, because many potential problems can be minimized during the class-composition period.

At the same time, parents appreciate an opportunity to give input into the selection of their child's teacher for the upcoming school year, and principals avoid accommodating such opportunities at their peril. An impromptu process promotes suspicion, because confusion regarding process creates the perception that the squeaky wheel gets the grease. A formal announcement ensures transparency and removes this potential irritant.

In one school district, each year around the time that class lists were being prepared, parents would receive notification via the school newsletter that teacher-student pairing was underway. Parents could then take action they deemed appropriate in requesting special consideration for their child. This process provided administration with valuable insight regarding perceptions in their school community. A parent's response also opened lines of communication for meaningful dialogue with the school's administration.

A COMMON CREED

Tension is inevitable when students attempt to protect their own interests by blaming someone else for their problems. Teachers may blame parents when issues in the home interfere with a student's ability to complete homework assignments, return documents, or arrive to school on time, with adequate clothing and materials. Later, when home at the dinner table, the child may negatively embellish correctional actions school staff took to manage their behavior. Children frequently shift blame to others rather than accept responsibility.

Therefore a periodic reminder in the school newsletter or during announcements when parents are in the school can remind everyone that two-way communication may be wiser than jumping to conclusions. The community can embrace a simple credo that instead of jumping to conclusions, holding out for explanatory information may be the wisest course when a student, seeking to protect themselves, is handing out blame liberally. The principal should offer parents, "I won't believe everything your child says about you if you won't believe everything your child says about us"—which quickly reminds everyone how easily issues can be misconstrued, while also likely getting a ready chuckle from any adults in the room.

PARENT VOLUNTEERS

School principals should work to bring parents into the school to assist with various classroom activities, and school procedures should be a deliberate focus. Schools have successfully energized parental interest and assistance in a number of ways:

- *Artistic talent:* One parent gifted in oil painting depicted numerous Disney characters playing different instruments along the school's walls. Subsequent school-repainting programs by the district worked around these murals, which remain more than three decades later.
- *Annual fund-raising efforts conducted by parent groups, featuring school-wide academics:*

  - *Student reading:* Parents met weekly with students who had read a book and conducted an interview checking comprehension. Parents were equipped with a list of questions they could use during the interview.
  - *Student spelling:* For a one-month period, weekly spelling tests for each grade were marked by parent volunteers, with student identifiers replaced with a number to ensure anonymity for the marker.
  - *Mad-minute facts:* For a one-month period, the students were asked weekly basic mathematic questions by parents, who used a prescribed set of facts to determine how many could reasonably be answered within a minute.

- *Coaching:* Parents gifted in music were invited to mentor students playing the recorder and handbells in music classes, and athletically gifted parents were asked to teach various skills in the sports program.
- *Driving students to other schools for competitions.*
- *Accompanying field trips as additional supervisors.*
- *Participating on the school's parent advisory council.*

These examples of ways to build a productive relationship between home and school can help overcome possible tensions arising from minor issues. While it is natural to expect that parents assume responsibility for ensuring positive relationships with their child's school personnel, the onus for building and maintaining support from the home should be shared by school staff. The suggestions provided in this chapter can help foster an environment where parental support is built and then maintained when conflicts arise.

These suggestions for involving parents pale in comparison with the suggestion offered in the next chapter. So basic is this concept that it is more readily identified as requisite for operation. The ongoing communication between a child's teacher and parents determines greatly whether the home/school relationship is built on trust.

Chapter Three

The Truth and Nothing But

Conversations between educators and parents regarding a child's success in learning is the paramount factor in efforts to bond home and school. We seek to do more than merely build a relationship. Our intent in this chapter is to explain how to create a trusting connection initiated by teachers as they communicate with their students' parents. Truthfully conveying a student's educational progress to the parents is essential to any teacher looking to build a meaningful relationship.

Equally important is the school's posturing when a student struggles to achieve grade-level standards of learning. Parents frequently feel that school personnel are pointing their fingers at them—pressuring the parents to provide more help in the home or to purchase additional educational services—when really parents just want to hear how the school will adjust to accommodate their child's difficulties.

Signaling that the student has learning difficulties is the first step. In one school district, at every reporting period, the principal or teacher conference focused on many aspects of each child's development; however, the priority issue pertained to the level of achievement in the core-curricular areas of language arts and mathematics. Specifically, the question was whether the student was achieving *at*, *above*, or *below* grade level. The answer to this assessment was always communicated to the parent. And most typically, parents responded to this information with appreciation: previous schools had rarely told them their child had been struggling academically, even though they may have suspected it all along.

Student achievement deemed *above* or *below* grade expectations required a plan of action for individualizing learning, and it was the principal's responsibility to ensure a plan was in place and results consistently monitored. Most students move from one teacher to another at the end of the school year or semester; however, the principal is the common link over a period of years. Therefore, in this school, principals partnered with many teachers in the educational development of each student, and participating in this partnership gratified teachers.

Making adjustments to a student's educational program also considers pace of learning in the core subjects deemed necessary for a basic education. Maturation matters, and some students cannot learn at the curriculum's pace. Many students fall behind simply because they are born in the later months of the school system's registration window, and their lack of maturity prevents them from keeping pace (Dueck, 2013).

Education systems have grappled with this reality for centuries but lacked data to adopt appropriate intervention. In the latter half of the twentieth century, *social promotion* became a popular strategy for dealing with struggling students, because many educators believed placement with age peers to be more appropriate than placement consistent with educational progress. Put simply, the question is, which is the preferred solution—retaining struggling students to repeat a course or grade level or socially promoting them so they can progress through their education with their peer group?

Today data demonstrate that the use of social promotion in the education system is endemic and injurious. Weaknesses in teachers' knowledge of and skill in assessing students and differentiating instruction pedagogies contribute to an erroneous perception regarding how children progress through our school system. The critical balance is disturbed between the competing approaches of social promotion and strict adherence required to meet grade standards. The former values placing students with age-appropriate peers, whereas the latter produces pass/fail accountability and attention to standards.

Schools originally emphasized student progress based on an ability to meet grade-level standards; however, difficulties arose when school attendance became mandatory to age sixteen and older. Too many students found it difficult to maintain pace with the grade curriculum and so were failed. Many students were actually failed more than once while pursuing graduation requirements.

Adopting a social-promotion approach for progressing students through the educational system has created a different set of problems for our schools. A principal in one school district explained his concern about low achievement among his middle-school students. After testing reading levels with the entire population of grade 9 students, the principal found that almost one-half were functioning at more than two grade levels below grade placement. Students were just being pushed through the school's program without appropriate intervention. Students were being taught English, but no one was teaching them to *read* it.

When working with students, a delicate balance must be stricken between using pass/fail accountability and social promotion. Too many students are merely pushed through the school system because social promotion is so dominant. Many schools have lost their zeal for ensuring that students meet grade-level standards. The evidence is most acute in our universities, which provide extensive remediation and preparation courses for students exiting high schools who are unable to cope with the academic workload. When working on the American Common Core standards in the Race to the Top initiative, U.S. educational leaders indicated that the average high school graduate in too many states was achieving only grade 10 standards.

The imbalance given to social promotion has wrought enough damage in North America's school systems. Although a few students with special needs are unable to progress based on achievement, and therefore require social promotion, the rest of the student population is capable of bolstering grade-level achievement. However, the current predicament is not unlike the manipulation used by school districts in the late twentieth century, when approximately 20 percent of American students were excused from writing system-wide tests over concern that tests were too difficult.

This "continuous-pass" orientation has had a significant effect on the educational system. Decades ago, Cunningham and Owens aptly summarized the effects of this trend. "Social promotion," they wrote, "is accomplishing what it was intended to do: it is relieving the various grades of overage, floundering students. If we are to help these potential failures, we must devise new educational systems" (1976, n.p.). According to the United States' National Center for Education Statistics (2006), in 2004 only 9.6 percent of youth ages sixteen to nineteen had been retained in a grade at some point. This represented a decrease from 16.1 percent in 1995—a reduction of 6.5 percentage points, or 40 percent.

Thompson and Cunningham (2000) summarized the considerable confusion evident at the apex of the social-promotion movement:

> The issue of whether it is better to retain low-performing students in grade or to pass them along with their age-mates has been both hotly disputed and heavily studied for decades. Advocates of retention have maintained that it sends a message to all students that weak effort and poor performance will not be tolerated, and that it gives lagging students an opportunity to get serious and get ready for the next grade. Opponents have argued that retention discourages students whose motivation and confidence are already shaky, and that promoted students gain an opportunity to advance through the next year's curriculum, while retained students go over the same ground and thus fall farther behind their advancing peers.

Part of the confusion is conveyed in the last line—*retained students go over the same ground*. It is poor practice for any teacher to expect the same pace for all learners. During the school year, relatively little adjustment would have been made to accommodate the struggling students, and at the conclusion of the year, *these students were declared failures*. In other words, the students then started school the next year at the same place as they had a year earlier and *repeated* the curriculum. This method for dealing with struggling learners is a pedagogical failure.

Some schools utilized a different approach, where students do not go over the same ground when repeating a year. *They never failed, but they were retained*. In one school, as soon as teachers detected that a student was falling behind, individualized programming was put into place, and the instructional pace for that student was adjusted. Usually falling behind one year in the curriculum took more than one year in school to make up, or else it was the case that the student had started the school year already deficient in intellectual maturation. In effect, this school was shouldering the responsibility that ensured this learner succeeded.

When a student fell more than a year behind peers, the school, in consultation with parents, made a decision to *retain* the student with a younger group. Frequently the additional year of intellectual maturity allowed for a normal pace of learning from that point, but the student would neither experience gaps in instruction from social promotion nor the repetitive teaching used in the failed approach. Grade-level standards were the key factor in student-placement decisions.

Social promotion disregarded the poor practice of failing and the more acceptable practice of retaining, the defining feature of which is that students remained with age-appropriate peers with an expectation that teaching will be adjusted to accommodate the learner. Intellectual maturation necessary for successful progress could remain a problem.

Thompson and Cunningham (2000) discussed the merits of both approaches:

> Overall, neither social promotion nor retention leads to high performance. If the goal is to bring low-performing students up to the higher standards now being asserted across the nation, neither retention nor social promotion is effective. In different studies, one or the other has been found to offer an advantage, but neither has been found to offer a large, lasting advantage, and neither leads to high performance.

Soon after Thompson and Cunningham published their findings, reaction against social-promotion policies recorded by the nonprofit organization Public Agenda (2001) demonstrated the attitudinal shift taking place across the U.S. school system:

> The number of teachers who say their own schools practice social promotion has dropped from 41 percent to 31 percent over the last four years, according

to a new nationwide survey by nonpartisan, nonprofit Public Agenda. *Reality Check 2001*, which surveys teachers, parents, students, employers, and college professors on standards in their community, was published in today's issue of *Education Week*. It also shows an increase in summer school attendance and more positive attitudes among parents about standards in public schools.

Public Agenda went on to explain how the change in attitudes regarding use of social promotion was changing practices in schools. The number of teachers reporting student attendance in summer school jumped from 28 percent one year to 37 percent four years later. Further, the number of teachers who said that students now take summer school seriously rose to 53 percent, an increase of ten percentage points since 1998.

A positive spin-off on parental attitudes was also reported, demonstrating that social promotion had been controversial with them. The number of parents saying that local public schools have higher standards than local private schools rose from 22 percent in 1998 to 34 percent at the time of the survey, while the number of parents saying private schools have higher standards fell from 42 percent four years prior to 35 percent. Parents began supporting the shift toward higher standards in public schools.

The debate between social promotion and retention has produced a difference of opinion regarding research methodology. As reported in a 2011 white paper by the National Association of School of Psychologists, some researchers argued that same-grade comparisons are more consistent with the purpose of retention, which is to provide students the opportunity to be more successful in meeting the academic demands of future grades (relying on findings from Karweit, 1999; Lorence, 2006).

This white paper provides a meta-analysis of studies of these educational approaches that reinforces retention as a more productive strategy than social promotion:

> A recent meta-analysis of 207 achievement effects nested in 22 studies published from 1990 to 2007 (Allen, Chen, Willson, & Hughes, 2009) determined that studies that used higher quality controls for selection effects (i.e., preretention differences between students selected for retention intervention and promoted peers) resulted in less negative effects for retention. (National Association of School of Psychologists, 2011, p. 2)

The white paper further indicated that:

> Although retaining students who fail to meet grade-level standards has limited empirical support, promoting students to the next grade when they have not mastered the curriculum of their current grade, a practice termed social promotion, is not an educationally sound alternative. For these reasons, the debate over the dichotomy between grade retention and social promotion must be replaced with efforts to identify and disseminate evidence-based practices that

promote academic success for students whose academic skills are below grade level standards. (p. 1)

Patricia Hawke (2006) examined results in Florida schools, which had begun moving away from a reliance on social promotion as an improvement strategy.

> The findings of the Florida schools' study showed that the performance gain of the retained students in 2002 exceeded that of the socially promoted students in 2001. The improvement gains were moderate in reading, yet significant in mathematics. The results were consistent in both the FCAT and Stanford-9 tests, showing the gains were due to student skill mastery rather than prepping.

Greene and Winters (2011) later provided their perspectives on Florida's reform effort and gave additional support for the use of retention as opposed to automatic promotion:

> Previous studies examined retention based on educator discretion. In a new study we conducted for the Manhattan Institute that avoids the pitfalls of earlier research, we find that holding low-performing students back helps them academically. We examined a policy in Florida that required third-grade students to perform at a certain level on the state's reading test to receive an automatic promotion to fourth grade. Students who performed below the required level and repeated third grade made significantly greater academic progress than similar students who were promoted despite their lack of skills. The benefit of being retained grew so that by the end of the second year the retained students entered fifth grade knowing more than the promoted students did leaving fifth grade — this despite the fact that the retained students had not yet been exposed to the fifth grade material.

In New York City, another school system working to adopt system accountability for student success, also shifted away from social promotion. McCombs, Kirby, and Mariano (2009) reported on that city's policy for assisting students who were falling behind:

> The policy places considerable emphasis on identifying struggling students early, providing them with additional instructional time, and continuously monitoring their achievement. Students who have been identified as in need of services at the beginning of the school year (based on their performance on the previous year's assessments, teacher recommendations, or being previously retained in grade) are mandated to receive academic intervention services (AIS) in school. In addition, schools can offer a variety of out-of-school support services, including Saturday school (previously called Saturday Preparatory Academies). Students who fail to score Level 2 or higher on the mathematics or ELA assessments administered in the spring are offered several opportunities to meet the promotion standards and can be promoted based on (1) a review of a portfolio of their work in the spring, (2) performance on the

summer standardized assessment, (3) a review of a portfolio of their work in August, or (4) an appeal process. Students who do not meet the standards when their portfolios are reviewed in the spring are required to enroll in the Summer Success Academy, which offers additional hours of intensive instruction in mathematics and ELA for several weeks in the summer. (pp. xxi–xxii)

When it came time to report on the results, McCombs et al. indicate this school system's success while accepting responsibility for helping their students succeed:

Scoring at the proficiency level (Level 3 or higher) in NYC schools has increased dramatically, while the percentage of students scoring Level 1 has declined equally dramatically. This same trend was evident across the rest of the state as well. (McCombs et al., 2009, pp. xxiv–xxv)

Examples of the findings of McCombs et al. (2009) follow:

Mathematics in grade 7 from 2006 to 2008

- Level 3 (Proficiency): improved by 25 percentage points
- Level 1: declined to 3 percent

English language arts in grade 5 from 2006 to 2008

- Proficiency: improved 17 percentage points.

It appears likely that these improvements are related to the set of reforms enacted by the city and state in the No Child Left Behind context. We also found no negative effects of retention on students' sense of school belonging or confidence in mathematics and reading over time. The near-term benefits we found hold out the possibility of longer-term benefits as well.

The RAND Corporation (Kirby et al., 2009) reviewed the New York City policy's results. "Administrators," RAND found, "reported that the promotion policy focused the instructional efforts of schools, made parents more concerned about student progress, and provided additional resources to support low-achieving students. Overall, retained students did not report negative socioemotional effects."

The underlying point in this research is that much of our educational system adopted social promotion as the dominant strategy for dealing with students experiencing difficulty in achieving more normal academic progress. It was the most common alternative to failing students rather than a better, but costlier, alternative dedicated to *early identification* of those students not meeting grade expectations and dedication to the provision of individualized, accelerated instruction utilizing evidence-based practices and frequent monitoring of progress.

Rather than consider these alternatives, most educators until recently have preferred to base their decisions on a flawed methodology in measuring retention, believing that social promotion was at least an improvement on any alternative. *Doing something*, so the wisdom went, *was better than doing nothing, even if the something wasn't really all that helpful either.* Believing that the social-promotion approach represented a legitimate strategy, educational leaders accepted it, thinking themselves off the hook. Many actually believed they were demonstrating compassion and responsibility, assuming the struggling students' needs were being met in being promoted with their age-peer group.

Call it *continuous pass* or *all pass*, either way, the social-promotion approach remains far too encompassing. Some students with exceptional needs are unable to achieve standards, but applying this approach to a large percentage of the student population changes the culture of the educational system—for the worse. Not only are expectations lowered, but neither do higher achievers have their needs adequately addressed, because attention and resources are increasingly directed toward those falling behind their age group (Dueck, 2013; Xiang, Dahlin, Cronin, Theaker, & Durant, 2011).

In order to assess social promotion and its relationship to the current practice of organizing students into age-based, single-date entry cohorts, it is helpful to look at the context giving rise to the system: adults establish schools and the entire educational superstructure in which they operate; their memories of childhood and life experience supposedly make them suitable architects of a world in which they no longer live.

But today's educational system is not our grandparents' educational system. Certain rules such as entry date have remained the same, but important practices in our schools have changed over time. For example, when educators began to face universal participation, they initially failed students who fell behind their grade placement. A 2009 article in the Canadian *Globe and Mail* (Mahoney, 2007) touched on the experiences of the Edmonton public school district as they pertained to this issue:

> The realization crept up on Edmonton school administrators and shocked them to the core: One in five children was failing grade 1.
>
> It was the early 1980s and officials learned of the high retention rate by chance through a testing program that found that about 20 per cent of pupils, many of them boys whose birthdays fell just before the enrolment cut-off, were in their second year of grade 1.

Failing students certainly was common in those days, and birth month, especially for boys, was a significant factor.

The newspaper article went on to explain that by 2007, across Canada, holding children back had become increasingly rare. Instead, children who failed to meet minimum grade standards usually moved ahead with their peers; in other words, they were being socially promoted. It arose out of well-intentioned compassion for children, who were thought to suffer poor self-esteem were they held back. Studies seemed to suggest that students would be more successful in school if they remained with age-level peers.

Consequently, teachers have grown reticent to be the bearers of bad academic news to parents of struggling students. As a result, parents remain ignorant of the situation, and the relationship between the teacher, the school, and the parents remains cordial and artificially productive. If the issue were simply one of producing a consumer product or of providing a nonessential service, the lack of transparency would still be problematic but the consequences not so tragic. The lines of communication between teachers and parents need to be open and characterized by informed integrity. Why? One superintendent explained it this way: We need to change the system because the system is supposed to be here to serve the kids.

Many school administrators today willingly acknowledge their school's efforts to give greater priority to uplifting the educational needs of weak students over enriching strong students. Essentially, this focus disadvantages stronger students. During our focus groups with educational leaders, they described situations where the stronger students spin their wheels because *teachers have become so focused on meeting the needs of weaker students* that they no longer have the time and the energy to address the needs of stronger students.

This unfortunate reality of minimizing the educational needs of talented students prompted administrators to comment that students experiencing behavioral problems were bright students who were not having their needs met; in the colorful language of one principal, stronger students are nails that stand up, and teachers hammer them down, leading to rebellion.

This chapter is devoted to examining the bond established between parents and school and particularly considers the research pertaining to social promotion, a waning trend in dealing with struggling students. Our school district did not have a policy regarding how to deal with struggling students, choosing instead to identify each principal as the decision maker for their community. In my experience, school districts have benefitted when parents have reinforced the trend to move away from social advancement toward a practice of allowing the schools to advise parents of appropriate academic placement for their child *while also* working to ameliorate the child's academic deficiencies. We'll discuss this further in chapter 6.

Chapter Four

Bonding with Students

The previous chapters provide strategies for bonding school and home, which is important because there are occasions when negative community chatter may hinder a school's success. High levels of student satisfaction about their school tend to overcome most negative undercurrents, because parents appreciate hearing children's excitement about their school. The importance of building a positive school climate can never be overemphasized.

Classroom teachers are responsible for building productive relationships with students for effective instruction. There is also considerable time when students are in school but outside the classroom teacher's watchful eye and influence. This chapter provides strategies for effectively managing the school by building strong relationships with students.

ASSEMBLY BEHAVIOR

Bringing the student body together invites noisy and potentially rowdy behavior, while managing these events can increase the students' level of pride in the school. Once, upon inheriting a principalship where staff were displeased with student behavior during assemblies, we purposed to make the event a positive experience from the moment students left their classroom until they returned. A simple motivational strategy generated the students' overwhelming cooperation, and word spread, bringing many from the outside community to see for themselves.

We leveraged the children's love of the school mascot to motivate good behavior in this way: Students were observed from the moment they left their classrooms and as they traveled through the halls, entered the auditorium, and waited for everyone else to take their places. Almost immediately—and each year following—truly absolute silence dominated throughout the school to such a degree that soon the back of the auditorium contained many parents, guests from other schools, and central-office personnel, all wanting to observe the phenomenon for themselves. The principal's watchful eye assessed the conduct of each class entering the auditorium, while they waited for the arrival of other classes and to participate in the program. Then, once each assembly had concluded, and students had quietly returned to their classrooms, an announcement identified which well-behaving classroom would be the mascot's "home" until the next assembly—a reward the students were eager to attain. In setting up this behavior-reward system, a significant corner was turned with out-of-control student behavior, and the students' greatly improved conduct remained consistent—until a new principal, with a different perspective, was installed.

Extrinsic motivation may not be everyone's tack. However, its use can achieve desired results when adopted consistently and fairly; in the case of this school, using a single award was sufficient to motivate 500 students in a very tough community. That said, additional award symbols may be necessary for larger schools or to inspire greater motivation.

BELONGING TO A TEAM

Anyone with experience of playing on a team understands the excitement generated by group success and the camaraderie experienced through group loss. Learning how to be a contributing member of a team is an important life skill enhanced through ongoing practice, and students are better prepared for life's work when they learn teamwork early in life. Experience with coaching young children demonstrates how challenging it can be for one player to go beyond a "me" mentality to a "we" mentality. Schools can enhance sense of team beyond student participation in sports teams.

Utilizing a house-league structure in some schools, we have placed all students on a team identified by a name or color, awarding team points for numerous activities, like:

- Sports-day events
- Seasonal intramural sports activities
- Weekly spelling tests
- Weekly basic-facts tests
- Current-events tests, appropriate to grade level
- Geography quizzes
- School fund-raising
- And incorporating a number of other activities that could fit into the team structure.

Scoring points can be tabulated on a per-student basis when the team members are evenly distributed; however, a simple mathematical calculation can use the average per-person score in the school or class.

Spirit days, when students are encouraged to wear their team's colors, provide opportunities for bonding between classes and grades. Whether this translates to a friendly wave between team members walking the school's hallways or a brief exchange on the playground, identifying with a team member contributes to school spirit. These spontaneous reactions forge relationships between different ages, instilling a greater sense of care for the community.

Incorporating this sense of team spirit in many aspects of the school's program also stimulates interest in multiple curricular areas, because we make sure that recognition goes beyond athleticism. Opportunity for contributing to team success motivates additional individual effort in academic programs because most students feel a sense of obligation to support their teammates.

GENERATING APPROPRIATE STUDENT BEHAVIORS

Student misbehavior is always a school issue, regardless of the demographic area served. Yes, regional differences will translate to different cultural expectations for what constitutes good behavior, but there is such a thing as unmistakable student wrongdoing, and it can and must be managed. Capacity to manage this concern was recognized when the superintendent offered a new administrative appointment and prefacing the opportunity with the statement, "We are giving you a change to a more moderate environment before sending you back into a tough school." With the exception of the two years this school administrator ended up spending at that school, thirteen years of a fifteen-year career of administrative leadership had been spent serving the school district's inner city and lowest socioeconomic communities.

The last school placement that administrator received was in a community so impoverished that telephone booths had to be installed for residents who had no home phones. While today's technology makes this specific plight less relevant, community poverty and many of the social needs stemming from poverty remain a concern for school administrators. As in so many underserved communities, this administrator had to resolve behavioral issues requiring immediate attention; in many cases, teachers found that a home visit satisfactorily resolved specific student misbehaviors, and subsequently student misbehavior in general was reduced by this personalized effort. Sitting together at the kitchen table proved to be more effective than speaking on the telephone.

In the end, in this particular school, home visits put the teachers at too great a personal risk, but even so, we found that many doors were opened by the school's commitment to forging positive personal relationships with the parents—like during the family fun nights. In fact, the students' improved behavior at school reflected the school's strengthened relationship with the home, and seldom were additional visits required. It is debatable whether this strategy of home visits would work in a community where a consistent effort hadn't already been made to connect the school with the wider community—like through the personalized notes from the principal, family fun nights, AGMs, and the other strategies outlined in chapter 2. The proverbial pump must be primed for a home visit to be welcome.

Recognizing that visiting students' parents at home may not always be workable or safe for a teacher, nonetheless, management of irresponsible student behavior remains a basic requirement of the job. In one school, teachers said that when faced with serious classroom misbehavior they did not wish for their principal to assume teaching a scheduled class. Rather, the teachers wanted an immediate response to a call for administrative support for repeating or serious student misbehavior. And so the protocols were established such that a quick intercom buzz to the office usually produced a rapid response even while the issue was still escalating.

Consequences for poor student behavior must be immediate, and consequences for episodic misbehavior must be progressive, and always appropriate. In one school, a centralized file was opened for every student whose behavior had required administrative intervention. This record contained a brief summary of misbehaviors, including the student's ownership of a concern as well as the mutually agreed consequence, which also served as a discussion point in subsequent referrals. A psychological benefit is triggered when recalcitrant behavior is reviewed with the student, which facilitates breaking their chain of poor behaviors.

Identifying appropriate consequences is also key to generating acceptable behaviors among students. Mores fluctuate over time, but the consequences have included:

- Having the student serve detention at recess or after school, with the student facing a wall, and the detention time being extended any time the student interacted with another student
- Having the student pick up garbage from the playground for a specified period of time, with a staff member assigned to examine the clean-up to ensure accountability
- Having the student perform a routine activity for the school's custodian
- With incidences of fighting, having involved students privately discuss the differences that had initiated the conflict, as well as identifying more

productive reactions to similar situations and presenting resolutions for maintaining a peace
- Observing the student's appropriate behaviors on the playground and writing a report that relates to the student's misbehavior and that must be presented to the administrator; depending on the situation, the report, which becomes part of the student's behavioral file, could be written after school or at home, in which case the parent would cosign
- Having the student sign a behavior contract, witnessed by the parents, which summarize the concerns, solutions employed, and the covenants made
- Applying corporal punishment to the student
- And, failing all of the above measures, suspending the student—ideally where the school district, or grouping of regional schools, operates a suspension class for chronic misbehaviors, and with the school providing work or assignments for the student to complete while assigned to the suspension class or to complete privately if serving the suspension at home.

Fluctuating mores are especially evident concerning the use of corporal punishment as an alternative to suspension. Clark (2017) reported that, "Nationwide, it's not unusual for parents to support the use of corporal punishment as a form of discipline. Recent surveys show about 75 percent of Americans believe it's sometimes necessary to spank a child."

Corporal punishment has a distinct advantage over suspension because the student avoids being penalized academically. An imposed holiday from school for a student already not wishing to be there is not well served by a suspension; we want every student to be present for instruction every day, and abetting an absence is counterproductive. Corporal punishment immediately concludes the issues leading to the consequence without impeding the student's opportunity to return to a learning environment.

Currently, controversy surrounds this disciplinary practice because some people equate corporal punishment with beating. "According to the Center for Effective Discipline," McGuire (2016) reports, across the United States,

> the 19 states that still allow corporal punishment are largely concentrated in the South, Southwest, and the Midwest. These states allow teachers and school administrators a pretty loose definition of how they are able to dole out discipline. Another 31 states nationally have banned the practice of spanking students in schools, despite the 1977 Supreme Court ruling of *Ingraham v. Wright*, that found spanking in schools does not violate a child's rights. Some urban school districts like Houston, Memphis, and Atlanta still allow the practice of paddling as a form of discipline. Even in states that don't allow paddling, like Maryland, teachers have been found to spank or paddle children as a form of punishment.

The actions school administrators employ when disciplining students provide parents with a model for disciplining their children at home. Consequences are most effectively applied when they progress in severity and incorporate options from which the child can select. Modeling a low-level of emotions throughout the school's disciplinary process provides parents with examples of how they might discipline children in their home.

While a table of escalating consequences is necessary to promoting appropriate student behavior, an ongoing commitment by administrators must also be made to work on minimizing behavioral concerns, especially when settling students for learning is required. Every occasion when the student body enters the school, one of the entry points should be covered by the principal. Nothing needs to be verbalized, because the watchful gaze accompanied with occasional smiles, winks, and verbal praise produces amazing results. Consistently and persistently rotating through the entrances maximizes the principal's visibility.

Student activity on the playground also benefits from additional supervision without assigning school staff to the task. Leadership opportunities for older students to act as playground monitors for younger ones not only reduces misbehaviors by the younger but provides leadership development for the older. Younger students readily comply with instructions and verbal disciplining from older peers organizing games and activities on their behalf. Indeed, in our experience, correction from another student produced better response and results than correction from faculty or staff.

Success with student monitors led to another student-leadership approach within the instructional environment. On a weekly basis, all older students mentored a younger student for an hour in various learning activities—among them:

- Listening to them read and asking comprehension questions
- Reviewing basic facts
- Reviewing spelling words
- Assisting with various mathematics operations and problem-solving
- Geography study
- Reading to them and asking comprehension questions
- Assisting them in developing their library skills
- Solving puzzles for enrichment
- And assisting in writing poetry or short stories.

These buddy arrangements lasted for the term unless abrogated by an unanticipated difficulty. Watching these positive interactions between buddies then transfer to the playground was a benefit to the school as well as a nurturing friendship for students.

Occasionally, an elementary and middle school shared the same grounds and provided opportunities for the middle school students to buddy with older elementary school students. These upper elementary school students were buddying with primary grade students but were recipients of educational assistance from a buddy in the middle school. This arrangement was made possible through the middle school's options program and operated similarly to the description provided earlier—with consistent weekly interactions.

Finally, student attitudes toward their school can be influenced negatively when anonymous actors degrade school grounds. Graffiti is a malicious act against the people in the building, and the problem must be rooted out before it gets worse. Catching the perpetrator and exercising appropriate consequences will curtail the problem; however, addressing the concern must avoid wrongful accusations that would lead to a severed relationship. It would be logical to assume that graffiti inside the school is the work of a student, whereas graffiti on the outside of the building could be the work of anyone in the community—not just a student.

One school employed and perfected a technique to quickly and reliably identify the specific student who had defaced the grounds while mitigating the danger of ever wrongfully accusing an innocent student. Scrutinizing the formation of letters in the words for distinctive patterns was the first task. Constructing and administering a current-events test, or some other exercise using written responses, to students in classrooms most likely housing the violator was the next step.

The purpose for the test was never revealed to the students but, rather, was designed to appear to be a normal part of the ongoing classroom programming. Matching the students' script patterns from the testing instrument with the graffiti reliably indicated student guilt. A specific question in this confrontation with the identified student always generated the confession. When confronting the guilty party, asking "Why did you do this?" rather than "*Did* you do this?" reduced the likelihood that a student would attempt to lie. We avoided wrongfully accusing students, and the vandalization problem was immediately resolved, because the perpetrator had been quickly identified and so was unlikely to repeat the offense.

This chapter underscores a fundamental axiom of school leadership: *As the principal goes, so goes the school.* Teachers are responsible for managing their classrooms, but the principal can set a tone throughout the school that enhances students' respect and cooperation. Once a productive overall school climate is established, the principal can focus on the practices and learning conditions within each classroom.

Chapter Five

Teacher Supervision and Development

School administrators must be wary about their potential preoccupation with school management. Building schedules and timetables, purchasing supplies and educational resources, managing recalcitrant students, smoothing relationships with irate parents, keeping a watchful eye on the budget, and responding to the myriad requests from the central office for information are examples of how school administrators can have their attention deflected from a significant responsibility.

Managing a school is important work and, if neglected, creates substantial problems. Workers want an orderly environment, and teachers can be quickly distracted from their main responsibility of educating students if the management tasks are neglected. Staff morale is threatened when the operational base of the organization is in disarray, and, in school, the principal's career can end quickly when the management tasks are not appropriately addressed.

An emphasis on management poses a threat to leadership because schools are more than a business. Employees of any shopping center are required to know their products and use their personalities to establish a rapport with customers. Usually they restrict their focus to a single client, and the transaction is completed within minutes. Of course, the business community has many levels of complexity that require advanced skills and, without going into extensive detail, reward employees accordingly and considerably above the pay levels available to teachers.

Teachers deal with dozens of children at the same time whose attention spans vary considerably, as do their skills, abilities, and maturity. Students arrive in the classroom with a myriad of emotional issues, such as hormonal changes, family conflict and breakups, and ever-changing relationships with friends. Equally challenging for teachers is their need to compete for their students' attention in an electronic environment full of action, color, and noise. These issues and many more must be considered for approximately 200 days a year before a new set of clients arrive.

When a teacher is hired, there is no guarantee that their talent will produce the same levels of success in subsequent years or decades. Some will leave teaching, return to university for additional training, attend local workshops, go into administration, or simply stop doing the same thing day after day after day. The point is that ultimately the employer—and specifically their representatives, in this case, the principal—has a responsibility to enhance the success of their employees.

It is in fulfilling this responsibility to develop teacher talent that the principal moves from *manager* to *leader*. Presumably the school district's decision to promote someone to principal was based first and foremost on their assessment that the individual was an outstanding classroom practitioner and excellent model. Crossing the threshold from manager to leader still requires a *mind-set followed by action*.

The previous chapter demonstrated how a principal can influence a school climate conducive to quality learning in classrooms. This chapter demonstrates how a principal accentuates the school's success within the walls of each classroom, demonstrating once again that as the principal goes, so goes the school. In other words, accountability replaces absolute trust with an expectation that trust must be earned, and numerous strategies for enhancing teacher talent follow.

TRACKING SUPERVISION

Supervision is a loaded term, because it implies a lack of trust. *Withdrawing supervision implies absolute trust.* These two perspectives provoke controversy and so must be reviewed more diligently in public-sector enterprises, including education, where bottom-line thinking is less discerning than it is in the private sector. Those under supervision may grow suspicious if the supervision is applied inconsistently; therefore, this chapter outlines methods for normalizing supervision of staff.

Visiting each teacher at least once per week is an important goal for principals. Ensuring fairness in this supervision activity is equally important and managed by maintaining a list of staff with a record of visits recorded for each week. By itself, the recording process is revealing because of the questions it prompts. For example, why was a certain teacher's class not supervised by the principal? Are there other occasions when this class was not visited, and, if so, why did these omissions occur?

Benefits from this supervision process are significant. Whereas the research literature says that many teacher's classrooms are never visited by administration, yet my experience demonstrates that teachers actually appreciate a visible administration. The principal's constant "dip-sticking" of the learning environment in every classroom ensures a more comprehensive understanding of what is happening throughout the school. These observations help identify common concerns or needs for school-wide emphasis as well as which teachers might provide valuable leadership upon receiving the right development.

Equally important is the opportunity after a classroom visit for a principal to provide teachers with a positive comment reinforcing some aspect of effective teaching. Using a personalized notepad, a quick stop into the office to pen a succinct comment reinforcing a specific talent observed strengthens the teacher's commitment to further developing and utilizing that expertise. Implicit in this reinforcement of the teacher's talent is a message that the administrator is knowledgeable of the elements comprising effective teaching. In other words, teachers recognize a principal's knowledge of effective teaching practices.

These frequent classroom stop-ins have an added benefit for students. Sadly, in some schools the principal's voice is more recognizable than the principal themselves. The school's public-address system cannot be the main means by which students get to know their principal. Indeed, these recurring brief appearances in the classroom provide an excellent opportunity for the principal to engage in informal chats with specific students. Quarterly meetings with teachers regarding the success of each student—which are outlined in chapter 6—keep principals updated on their students' development, providing opportunities for the principal to personally offer positive messages to individual students while sauntering through the class.

Defining what counts as a supervisory visit provides clarity for ensuring this informal activity is a success. A supervisory visit does not include picking up forms from classrooms or delivering a message to the teacher or students. Rather, a supervisory visit is purposeful when the principal takes a few minutes to observe the classroom—even when some students may not even be aware that a visitor is present, though the teacher will always be aware.

Implicit in this valuable use of the principal's time, in addition to avoiding disruption to class activity, is ensuring that the classroom is not the teacher's fiefdom. Everyone's attention is diverted when a classroom door swings open. Therefore, the supervision of teachers emphasizes an open-door policy unless a particularly noisy activity will disrupt other classes or a special class meeting is required to deal with a specific problem.

The frequency of these supervisory pop-ins also provides an opportunity to validate a teacher's talent observed during the evaluation cycle. Many teacher contracts dictate specific steps during the evaluation process which produce unusual activities. Canned lessons, which some teachers prepare for occasions when a formal evaluation is announced, may utilize exemplary strategies because considerable attention was taken preparing for the observation. Our intent during the supervisory role is to observe daily practice rather than something rarely used.

This supervisory function differs from the evaluation process frequently identified in teacher contracts, as it should. Evaluations are based on scheduled activities because the practitioner's career is at stake. Promotions, demotions, and changes in pay, as well as termination from employment, are all possible outcomes at the conclusion of the evaluation process. Formalized procedures for conducting evaluations are frequently defined in employment contracts or collective agreements and, therefore, will not be outlined here. The supervision process should never be compromised through formalization in collective agreements.

TEACHER BUDDIES

In some of the schools we work in, certain teachers are initially invited to participate in a buddy program, limited to two or three teachers in the same school. The commitment from each buddy is to observe the other teacher on a minimum of two occasions within a month and interact after each observation. Prior to the observation, the teacher being observed *could* request that their buddy focus on feedback to specific areas of focus, such as:

- The appropriateness of the number and degree of difficulty of questions posed to the students used during the lesson
- How specific students were involved
- Activity ratio and when some students began dropping out
- Pace of learning
- The teacher's checking for understanding
- Students' unobserved misbehaviors
- The teacher's movement throughout the classroom
- Teaching to the corners of the class
- Use of the voice to motivate learners
- Which students were not paying attention and when they lost their focus
- And charting eye contact with the teacher at specific intervals for specific students.

By asking the observing teacher to focus on these types of specifics, the threat of evaluation is removed. Asking the observing teacher to "just watch and give me feedback" is not a wrong approach, per se, but may require a minimal level of relationship between the teachers before it can be an effective kind of feedback. Therefore, the principal leading the teacher-buddies program should help add value to the assessments by suggesting things teachers can look for, and then allowing participants to broaden the scope as they see fit.

The teacher-buddy evaluations should be wrapped up in a meeting with the principal. Nothing should be recorded at this interview, and any notes prepared by the observing teacher should be given to the teacher who was observed. No official records are kept in order to ensure that this remains a low-risk activity that opens a classroom valuable feedback and provides the teacher with important information and insight. The principal understands that these teachers are interested in enhancing their skill as well as identifying what issues emerged during the discussions.

An alternative to buddying teachers within the school is allowing teachers to buddy outside of their schools. Partnering with specific friends who work outside of a teacher's own school may reduce the anxiety and hesitancy the teacher may feel about allowing someone else to observe their classroom; however, travel time complicates this additional option. It is also likely that the concluding conference with the principal will be only with the individuals in that same school. Nevertheless, this format is an option when anxieties run high.

Similarly, specialist teachers may not have an opportunity for meaningful evaluation from teachers qualified in their pedagogical area unless they go outside of their school. Though the logistical hurdles will arise, the benefit of observing and interacting with a related outside program makes this a worthy consideration.

ASSESSMENT BUDDIES

Assessing student work accurately is a critical skill for teachers, especially as students progress into higher grades and provide detailed written responses and reports. *Whenever subjectivity is involved, there is a chance that teacher bias can creep into the marking.* Unfortunately, the bias may be toward inflated marks because higher marks enhance students' opportunities to enter prestigious universities. Or inflating marks may cover up ineffective teaching or influence a more positive relationship between student and teacher.

Unfortunately, ample research demonstrates that grade inflation is rampant and that it more readily advantages female students because of their more compliant behavior (Dueck, 2017). A difficulty in addressing teacher bias is how many teachers are unaware of the problem. Bias may be subliminal and not readily discerned until we compare a teacher's marks with students' marks earned on standardized tests that were anonymously marked. Teacher bias is unfair to students and is so pervasive a problem in education that chapters 7 and 8 of this book provide extensive guidance for how a school system can identify and rectify it.

Encouraging teachers to participate in centralized marking for system testing provides an effective professional-development opportunity. In fact, where these opportunities are available, teachers should participate minimally every five years. A well-run marking session includes group practice and discussion using item responses with tests from previous years.

At the school level, principals can initiate in-services for teachers at an informal level. Encouraging teachers to buddy with other teachers of the same grade, regardless of the school, can provide a learning opportunity in assessing student work consistently. Teachers do not have to use the same assignment, though doing so may add value. Neither do they have to engage in the activity in the same place or at the same time.

After assigning students a project requiring written responses, the classroom teachers mark their respective students' assignments without displaying any marks or comments on the students' papers; however, they record these marks in their record book. The teacher then exchanges their class's papers for their buddy teacher to mark and record these marks separately and does the same in return for their buddy teacher. Having both sets of assignments marked by both teachers, marks are then compared for consistency. These teachers then discuss possible reasons for assignments with significant discrepancies. The conclusions from this comparison provide feedback to both teachers regarding their consistency and, indeed, whether they may be influenced by biases.

RESOURCE FORUMS

On a regular basis, teachers go to considerable effort to develop course units for their students. Designing these resources requires in-depth study of the curriculum to ensure that the academic objectives are covered at varying levels of difficulty and that the activities generate interest among their students. Finding sufficient time to develop a course unit during the school term is difficult because of the requirement for concentrated effort while the teacher's workload is already so significant. With so many other duties in a teaching day, motivation and energy to produce a dynamic instructional resource can lag.

Many teachers construct several classroom instructional units that promote personalized learning or, as it was previously called, *individualized learning*. Notably, prior to today's technology, one fully individualized mathematics program for several grades required approximately 1,000 hours of personal and volunteer time. Textual resources had to be cut and pasted onto recipe cards. Assessments had to be developed and wide-ranging enrichment activities incorporated.

When this instructional unit was fully developed and applied in the classroom, there was never an occasion when the entire class participated in the same lesson; rather, each student received countless mini-lessons weekly. Equally significant was a total absence of class disruptions for student misbehavior. With more than forty students in this mathematics class, everyone was on task all of the time, and the only noise heard was from a dialogue between the teacher and a specific student or from one student teaching another what they had learned a few days earlier. Indeed, so motivated were the students in this class that many would arrive thirty minutes before school and remain for thirty minutes after school so that they could progress at their rate through the kit.

Other teachers in the school were fascinated by the program and copied it for their own use or inherited the kit until years later when technology advanced to the degree that similar resources were readily available on personal computers. Reward came from walking into classrooms and observing students working through the kit then inherited and utilized by teacher colleagues.

This kit attracted the attention of teachers from other schools, and the degree to which they launched a similar resource is unknown. However, sharing resources—whether personally developed or commercially produced and then packaged into a more comprehensive resource—has motivation potential for all involved.

Therefore, school administrators exercise strong leadership through coordinating occasions when teachers from several schools bring their personally constructed units into a common display. Seeing a resource someone has developed not only stimulates new ideas but sparks people's sense of commitment to incorporating motivational learning resources with their own students. Even observing how some commercially produced resources are used in another teacher's classroom generates enthusiasm for personal exploration.

PROFESSIONAL DEVELOPMENT IS BUSINESS

Staff meetings are essential to the smooth operation of a school. There are many issues on the school's business agenda that need to be addressed, and these formal meetings provide opportunity for input as well as consistent communication among all staff. Some staff members may consider these meetings a necessary evil.

Staff meetings should also be used to provoke thoughtfulness about teaching and learning. Either at the beginning of the meeting or concluding with a brief presentation from a teacher on staff reminds everyone that teaching and learning are the primary functions of the school. At the beginning of the term, teachers should indicate at which scheduled meeting they will present an instructional idea they are using in their own classrooms. This simple strategy provides a constant flow of new ideas as well as motivation to explore in a new teaching concept for presentation to peers.

PROFESSIONAL-DEVELOPMENT SERIES

Good school leadership includes assessing educational needs evident throughout the school and then finding resources to address these concerns. Naturally, many opportunities are available through teachers' organizations locally as well as numerous conferences. Often forgotten, however, is the leadership role principals can assume while remaining in the school rather than incurring expenses traveling to other locations.

Back in the days of videotape, it was astonishing to see how many teachers in the school signed up for one principal's weekly lunch-hour session, comprised of watching a video and then engaging in a brief discussion. Depending on the length of the series, one or two series would be scheduled per academic year. Sharing experiences arising from the prior week's video would be followed by a discussion on the value and possibilities of the most recent video's lesson. This process was valuable for teachers because outsiders were not included, keeping the discussions honest: everyone could tell when someone was being unrealistic out of an attempt to be impressive.

Transferring this to our modern era, Internet capabilities mean online services for teachers abound. Principals can still play an important leadership role in their teachers' professional development by facilitating group viewings of these online segments followed by discussion; or, as a time-saver, teachers could preview the segment at their own convenience and then meet with the group and principal to discuss. The principal's involvement remains a key matter because their knowledge of the professional-development contents and the ensuing discussions provides an excellent focus while supervising teachers, as discussed earlier in this chapter.

FEEDBACK ABOUT STUDENT ACHIEVEMENT

It is inevitable that teachers receive feedback about the success of former students after the students have moved on to a different classroom in the same school. It is also likely that some information is exchanged informally in the staff room or while the teacher is perusing cumulative records available at the school until these records follow the student to a new school. Principals should formalize feedback when standardized-test results are returned to the school by ensuring that teachers see test scores for students they have recently taught. Requesting teachers to highlight unexpected achievement levels on these tests for previously taught students adds value to this process.

Principals should also ensure that information regarding student success flows back to teachers after students graduate to a feeder school. This information is valuable to the teacher. The principal should make sure to review all academic records, including standardized test scores, of previous years' students to ascertain how these results compare with the school's previous assessments. Tendencies for grade inflation must be monitored, which is more readily discerned when students move into regional schools with a larger catchment and a greater range of student abilities.

PRINCIPALS AS ROLE MODELS

Any person will suffer a degree of anxiety when called upon to give a demonstration to staff, and this is doubly true when it's the principal who is personally modeling the teaching. Assuming that the school district's fundamental principle for promoting a teacher to the position of principal is the teacher's excellence in the classroom, a considerable resource is created when a principal records their teaching and openly discusses it with their teachers. When the principal introduces this activity with a self-critique, including an analysis where best practice was not evident and encouraging teachers to indicate how the teaching could have been improved, a more relaxed environment for purposeful discussion is created.

Mutual trust is the key element for making this initiative successful. A supervisory environment outlined earlier builds the necessary levels of trust for teachers to freely express their opinions, and the principal's nondefensive response deepens this trust. Everyone is a learner because everyone is a teacher.

TEACHER PERCEIVER

Selecting and developing teachers is a key part of every principal's leadership responsibilities. I have been greatly aided in these functions in using a commercial tool built on all-inclusive research regarding effective teaching. The Teacher Perceiver Instrument from the Gallup organization ferrets out which candidates have the greatest classroom potential. The functionality of this instrument includes a provision for working with teachers individually by listening to their responses to a series of open-ended questions in twelve themes (Gallup Organization, 2002):

Thematic areas are:

Mission—Mission is what takes some individuals and groups out of society's mainstream in order to assure the quality and purposiveness of that mainstream. Mission is a deep underlying belief that students can grow and attain self-actualization. A teacher with mission has a goal to make a significant contribution to other people.

Empathy—Empathy is the apprehension and acceptance of the state of mind of another person. Practically, we say we put ourselves into the other person's place. Empathy is the phenomenon that provides the teacher feedback about the individual student's feelings and thoughts.

Rapport Drive—The rapport drive is evidenced by the teacher's ability to have an approving and mutually favorable relationship with each student. The teacher likes students and expects them to reciprocate. Rapport is seen by the teacher as a favorable and necessary condition of learning.

Individualized Perception—Individualized perception means that the teacher spontaneously thinks about the interests and needs of each student and makes every effort to personalize each student's program.

Listening—The listening theme is evident when a person spontaneously listens to others with responsiveness and acceptance. Listening is viewed as beneficial to the speaker.

Investment—The investment theme is indicated by the teacher's capacity to receive a satisfaction from the growth of the students. This is in contrast to the person who must personally perform to achieve satisfaction.

Input Drive—Input drive is evidenced by the teacher who is continuously searching for ideas, materials, and experiences to use in helping other people, especially students.

Activation—Activation indicates that the teacher is capable of stimulating students to think, to respond, to feel, to learn.

Innovation—The innovation theme is indicated when a teacher tries new ideas and techniques. A certain amount of determination is observed in this theme because the idea has to be implemented. At a higher level of innovation is creativity, where the teacher has the capability of putting information and experience together into new configurations.

Gestalt—The gestalt theme indicates the teacher has a drive toward completeness. The teacher sees in patterns—is uneasy until work is finished. When gestalt is high, the teacher tends toward perfectionism. Even though form and structure are important, the individual student is considered first. The teacher works from individual to structure.

Objectivity—Objectivity is indicated when a teacher responds to the total situation. This teacher gets facts and understands first as compared to making an impulsive reaction.

Focus—Focus is indicated when a person has models and goals. The person's life is moving in a planned direction. The teacher knows what the goals are and selects activities in terms of these goals.

The process involves taping an interview with the teacher, after which the principal codes the teachers responses for specific themes. When this listening phase is completed, the principal is then trained to reinforce the helpful aspects of the teacher's perspective and also frame follow-up questions with the teacher to help them focus on enhancing this perspective. The Teacher Perceiver Instrument is valuable in maximizing principal/teacher professional relationships. Indeed, the hours spent in personal conversations focusing on these important teaching themes made this strategy one of our most beneficial professional activities.

PERSONAL GOAL SETTING

Setting annual goals should be a requirement for all staff, while accountability should be ensured through discussions with the supervisor at both the beginning and conclusion of the academic year. In some instances, such as when reviewing data on student achievement, the year-end discussion will spill into the following school year to accommodate data collection and analysis from year-end standardized testing. Frequently, teachers need coaching to establish realistic goals because they are overly ambitious. It is not unusual for workers to put more emphasis on impressing their supervisors than on setting realistic markers for success.

Potential personal goals might include:

- Specific areas for personal professional development, such as teaching strategies or leadership style
- How the individual intends to use centralized services, such as consultants, program specialists, supervisory staff
- Involving parents in the classroom or school
- Personal visits to other classrooms or schools
- Reading about or researching new concepts
- Improving specific behaviors with specific students in the classroom or in the school, such as attendance
- Attendance at specific conferences
- Establishing a professional buddy relationship with another teacher of similar professional standing
- Producing a presentation for the benefit of colleagues, because best learning is through presenting
- Serving on specific committees within the school or district
- Buddying with another teacher at the same professional level for the purpose of exchanging student assignments to be marked, and then comparing one another's marks for discussion and analysis
- And, based on previously collected data:

- Projecting a goal for improving student achievement in specific concepts or subjects
- Improving attendance for class, school, or specific students
- Reducing suspensions or specific negative behaviors for specific students or groups of students
- And increasing students participation in specific voluntary functions, such as choirs, sports teams, and clubs

Preferably these goal-setting sessions are with the individual's direct supervisor; however, principals in large schools may have to share the task with other administrators. These discussions, in most instances, are with only one administrator; however, an additional consideration is to include the teacher's specific team leader or department head in the conversation.

Teachers fulfill a critical role in preparing our next generation. Their teaching talent in classrooms must always be a priority so that our students benefit from superior service regardless of the teacher's age. Everyone experiences occasions when stress reduces levels of performance, and this chapter identifies strategies for constantly reinvigorating teachers. Some may demonstrate consistently high levels of motivation; however, people commonly experience performance doldrums from time to time.

Principal leadership is the key for maintaining high levels of service in our schools, whether it be in developing and working with new teachers or assisting seasoned practitioners experiencing some disillusionment. As we have seen, in any school, as the principal goes, so goes the school. Principals supply leadership expertise to leverage maximum effort and professionalism from their teachers, and this compendium contains many proven tools for achieving classroom excellence.

The next chapter reveals a gold-standard initiative in teacher supervision. The initiatives already discussed are valuable strategies for improving teacher talent; however, the strategy outlined in the next chapter ensures even higher levels of student success. Teachers in every school identified this initiative as the most significant support provided by school administration.

Chapter Six

Grade Level of Achievement

The initial two years I spent on a teaching temporary contract were immediately followed by an administrative appointment in a small elementary school. While in this position and for every year and several schools thereafter until moving into central office positions, *grade level of achievement*—or GLA—became the driving force for individualizing students' education. Extensive knowledge regarding each student's intellectual, social, and emotional development was used to maximize the school's effort and success.

Thirteen years in five schools of successful practice with GLA produced convincing evidence that this administrative approach was transformative. The culmination occurred in my final year prior to moving into district office leadership when the superintendent in Calgary, with more than 200 schools, announced our school as the highest achieving in the district. The socioeconomic status of the school was near the lowest in the district, and yet students were achieving test results far above expectations.

After spending a day in the school, interviewing every member of staff on the reasons for the school's success, the superintendent announced his findings. Each interviewee had told him the same thing: Consistent use of the GLA process had coordinated the school's resources toward the specific educational needs of each student. School administration and teachers working closely together had monitored the success of each student and planned extensive communication with parents, ensuring their support. Even the teachers' consistent message to the superintendent related to the sense of team operating within the school.

The following is a description of the GLA process:

- For each of the four reporting periods in a school year and during a two-week window prior to the release of student report cards, the principal and classroom teacher reviewed the progress of each student.
- Special-needs teachers joined these meetings for reviewing their students.
- The principal maintained extensive notes on each student, reviewable by teachers, in the current as well as subsequent years.
- These notes contained information regarding the student's academic success, concerns about behavior and effort, contact with and support from the home, and results of standardized assessments, including psychological assessments.
- Planned interventions were recorded, as well as an assessment of previous interventions where applicable.
- *A numeric conclusion was made of the student's current grade level of achievement in language arts and mathematics.*
- Key messages for the student's parents were recorded.

A philosophical principle against *social promotion* underpinned this GLA process. We were committed to appropriate interventions where necessary as well as holding students accountable for their effort. Occasionally students were retained in their grade because they had fallen behind in their core curricular program. Frequently these retentions were made in the cases of students with special needs or immaturity associated with later birth dates (Dueck, 2013).

Projecting the actual grade level of achievement in core curriculum required a knowledge of the expectations for the grades bracketing the student's current placement within the academic program. While this explanation may sound complex to any teachers unfamiliar with the process, your doubts will quickly be erased by responding to a simple question: Thinking of a specific student in your class, can you indicate whether or not the student is achieving *below*, *at*, or *above* grade placement? Ask any teacher, and their facial expression immediately conveys how readily they now understand GLA. Teachers instinctively know the degree of success experienced by each student.

The concept is simple: A student may be physically located within a class of students in their fifth year of school (e.g., grade 5); however, the student may only be functioning at a grade 3 level. Similarly, some students in that same grade 5 classroom may be functioning at a grade 7 level. Anecdotal evidence suggests that a traditional class of grade 5 students is comprised of a spread of abilities ranging five grade levels. In other words, a typical grade 5 class has a range of student ability in mathematics or language arts from grades 3 through 7. The most extreme example from our data had, within one classroom, one student reading at the grade 2 level with another at grade 12.

Naturally in our school instruction was individualized for students, and the GLA process ensured that groups of students received classroom instruction commensurate with their achievement. The team—comprised of classroom teacher, principal, and resource teacher(s)—planned a program to accelerate the learning of weak students and challenge the strong. Eventually the discussion centered on what might be the student's most appropriate placement in the next term. Our key principle was that a student's academic placement would be decelerated or accelerated by no more than one year because, in most instances, this was sufficient to provide appropriate learning.

Honest communication with the parent was a second key principle. Communicating the GLA for each student at each term ensured that parents were well informed of their child's progress and of the school's plan. Any parent unable to attend the quarterly meeting with their child's teacher received a personal call, ensuring that the critical messages were reviewed. Later, Edmonton Public Schools followed a similar approach and actually developed a secure website where parents could follow their child's annual progress in core subjects.

Parents with children recommended for retention were shown the evidence, including intervention efforts by ancillary teachers. The detailed records from previous years of GLA discussions had already provided early warning that the pace of learning was overly challenging for their child. And so there were no surprises—except in the cases when a student came from a different school. In these instances, parents frequently expressed appreciation for our assessment, because we were actually confirming their own perception about their child's progress, despite an absence of warning from the previous school. Indeed, many parents expressed their frustration that previous schools had refused to place their child in more appropriate instructional settings.

This GLA process then was the foundational component of teacher professional development, because it focused extensively on the development of every child in every classroom. This effort is the teacher's primary responsibility, and success was more readily achieved by implementing a team approach.

Years later, when serving as a provincial administrator, another need related to teachers' professional development emerged. The advent of standardized testing revealed a significant weakness occurring when teachers assessed student achievement. Inconsistent assessments of student work revealed a pattern of inflated grades, providing students, their parents, and taxpayers with a false sense of achievement within the school system. As chief administrator for the provincial accountability program in education, I was tasked with informing the public and charting a course of action.

Chapter Seven

Teachers' Inconsistency When Assessing Students

The preceding chapters summarize initiatives in which I participated and perspectives I developed during thirteen years of school administration before assuming twenty-five years at the district and provincial levels. The remaining chapters in this book outline a mix of strategies employed and issues identified for making a positive contribution at these levels. Developing policy plays a more preeminent role when leadership for many schools and districts is the focus.

Evaluating student work is a major activity in teaching. While it is a legislated requirement, teachers naturally understand the value in constantly assessing student learning so that they can give feedback to the student, report to parents on their child's learning, report to the public on the extent of learning generally, and use the assessment to modify their future instruction. Assessment is so critical that the teacher's skill in evaluating student achievement requires constant verification and ongoing honing.

Most educators will express disbelief when reading this chapter, because few will acknowledge their role in providing inconsistent assessments of their students' work. The prevalence of this problem, however, makes it necessary to reveal its extent before indicating how it can be reduced. Indeed, the concern is sufficiently documented to indicate *unfairness to students*.

The remedy—standardized testing coupled with anonymous marking—is unpopular with teachers because of its potential for holding them accountable for their success in the classroom and their ability to assess students' work accurately and without bias. Fairness to students becomes the overarching concern. Failure to ensure fairness is an example of negative leadership.

Teacher unions' orchestrated efforts to discredit large-scale testing make it necessary to openly discuss this issue. The unions' active insistence that teachers' assessments of student learning are accurate must be verified so that the trust is deserved. If the evidence refutes such accuracy, then trust must be replaced with accountability. This chapter challenges teachers' capacity to perform consistently accurate assessments of student achievement.

In 2008, Richard Phelps addressed a world congress of educators with his findings about student evaluation. "There is abundant evidence that teachers' marks are a very unreliable means of measurement," he concluded. "A teacher's grades and test scores are far less likely to be generalizable than any standardized tests. . . . If an assessment system uses tests that are not standardized, the system is likely to be unfair to many candidates." He told the assembled educators, "We need standardized tests because each of us is a prisoner of our own limited experiences and observations."

Phelps opened Pandora's Box in referencing the likelihood for *unfairness*. Using this term to describe inconsistencies in marking provokes a significant backlash from unions. Criticism is one thing, they say, but to suggest that it results in *unfairness toward students* is something they would not want said publicly. Experienced educators likely understand the voracity of Phelps's charge that they are a *prisoner of limited experiences and observations*. Seldom do teachers observe each other in the classroom, exchange their students' tests and compare assessments, or participate in marking centers where student anonymity is ensured.

The stakes for the teaching profession are high if issues of inconsistency and bias are revealed. Inconsistent evaluations of student achievement recently surfaced as a major concern in the United Kingdom. Teacher unions were pressuring their government to abandon large-scale testing in favor of trusting teachers' capacity to accurately assess student achievement. The government established an expert panel to review the issue, and Bevan, Brighouse, Mills, Rose, and Smith (2009) recorded the panel's response to the request:

> A high level of accountability for each school is beneficial for everyone who has a stake in the education system: pupils, parents, schools and the taxpayer. The fact that we have strong accountability in the education system means that we can confidently devolve a lot of autonomy to schools and invest high levels of trust in teachers and school leaders. It would therefore be misguided to weaken accountability. . . .
>
> The accuracy and consistency of teacher assessment is improving; and whilst there are issues around variability of marking in tests, independently measuring pupils against national standards remains, in our view, the best way of providing objective information on the performance of each pupil and each school. (p. 4)

The implication in this report is that *trust follows accountability*. Blind trust is not useful to anyone, and, therefore, measuring pupils against national standards is best achieved by using an assessment independent from the student's school.

In the United States, consistency in evaluating student work is a long-standing concern. In the *Encyclopedia of Education*'s discussion of school grading systems (Guthrie, 2003) traced the root of concern regarding marking inconsistencies back to the beginning of the twentieth century: As more children remained in school beyond grade 5, a shift to percentage grading seemed a natural by-product for increased numbers of students. Inconsistent marks on assessments quickly became a concern.

This encyclopedia references a study in 1912 by Starch and Elliott, wherein teachers marked identical English papers. On the first paper, the range of marks was from 64 percent to 98 percent with a second paper ranging from 50 percent to 97 percent. This finding precipitated a similar study for mathematics, which demonstrated an even greater discrepancy, with teachers' marks ranging from 28 percent to 95 percent. It was evident from these early studies that teachers were applying a variety of *personal biases* while marking these papers.

These marking discrepancies lead to the use of another methodology for reporting, which made use of scales with larger ranges such as *excellent*, *average*, *poor*, and *failing*. This shift to ranges in marks was also the genesis for using letter grades A, B, C, D, and F. While these methods reduced variation in grades from the earlier practice of percentages, they did not resolve the problem of teacher subjectivity. These ranges merely masked discrepant marks that were less than 20 to 25 percentage points.

ASSESSMENT INCONSISTENCIES AND THE BELL CURVE

Combatting these problems led to the introduction of *grading on a bell curve, with its prescribed distribution of scores for each of the letter grades.* This *quota system* for each letter grade, also known as "grading on the curve," relieved teachers of the difficult task of having to identify specific learning criteria for each mark range. The focus was on *ranking* students rather than on *rating* students' learning relative to standards. In other words, teachers found it relatively easy to place students' papers in a *rank order*, from best to poorest.

Teachers could readily discern differences in quality of assignments from students within their class and, not having to apply standards, could assess each student's response relative to others. The difficulty teachers experienced was in assigning a value to the work that could be applied consistently by all teachers across the state, school district, or even within their own school. Over time, as teachers gained experience, they might eventually develop an understanding of expectations for a specific grade and stray away from using the quota approach. When this occurred, inconsistencies were magnified, because some teachers applied the quota while others focused on the standards.

This tendency toward bias and its negative result on students is the purpose for this chapter and the reason why large-scale testing and anonymous marking are necessary for a fair approach in assessing student achievement. When unfairness is detected, actions designed to ensure fairness must follow.

ASSESSMENT INCONSISTENCIES TODAY

After a century of dealing with this problem of subjectivity in assessment, it remains a dominant issue in education. Webber, Aitken, Lupart, and Scott (2009) summarize their findings:

> Student assessment is a contested educational issue in most of the Western world. . . . Teachers' weak understanding of fair assessment practices appears to be a barrier to student assessment being perceived as a positive educational endeavour. . . . Reporting to stakeholders clearly, accurately, and sensitively is among the most difficult and uncomfortable parts of student evaluation for teachers and, therefore, may result in student achievement not being reliably conducted, interpreted or reported. . . . Much research suggests that teachers in general are not proficient in student assessment practices in the Western world. . . . Further, principals are not strong in leading assessment and assessment historically has been missing from principal preparation programs.

Assessment is so critical in education and yet remains so poorly done that professional-development conferences for upgrading skills flourish. Bob Marzano, an educational researcher and assessment guru, demonstrated the extent of this issue at a conference involving two thousand educators in Atlanta on October 19, 2007. After posting on the screen a student's marks for ten assignments, Marzano requested that conference participates assign the students' work a final letter grade. Amazingly, participants markings ranged from 30 percent to 90 percent clearly indicating that inconsistency remains a significant barrier to fairness to students.

Jost (2002) compared the relationship of course grades to a standardized test score that is comparable across all schools, districts, and states. Data used in this study included public high school student records from one diverse state in the continental United States, along with corresponding exam score records from the College Board. The conclusion was that, "When comparing schools, it is not uncommon to see that despite seemingly equal grades, scores on achievement tests show great differences in the student populations" (n.p.). *Different assessment criteria are at play in classrooms and standardized tests.*

Harlen (2004) also undertook a systematic review of research on the reliability of teachers' assessment used for summative purposes. "The findings of the review," he concluded, "by no means constitute a ringing endorsement of teachers' assessment; there was evidence of low reliability and bias in teachers' judgements." These biases lead to *unfair* treatment of students because marks are their *currency* for obtaining scholarships and entry into universities. *Ultimately, students are winners or losers because of their teachers' specific biases.*

Harvey Craft, a retired teacher focused on assessment, blogged on September 24, 2014, that

> The business of determining student grades—whether on assessments or for final evaluations has always been problematic. . . . Absolute objectivity is not possible when humans are involved. To improve learning, teachers need to improve uniformity in what they do as compared with what other teachers do.

Uniformity, or consistency, when teachers mark student work remains a significant concern. In a regional study, consistency between teachers' assessments of student responses while marking provincial examinations was always monitored. Controls in place for these marking sessions ensure *student anonymity*, and each question is marked by *two teachers*. When their marks vary by more than one point on a five-point scale, a third marker is involved.

Extensive training takes place prior to the marking process, and markers break from their task *twice daily* to review their standards by scoring a "reliability review" paper. The group compares individual assessments and discusses reasons for mark variances. The commitment for achieving consistency *is well beyond* what occurs within any school, because scholarships and placement into prestigious university programs are at stake.

Even when there is so much effort toward achieving consistency in assessing students' written responses, approximately 25 percent of upper-stream English, 12 percent of upper-stream social studies, and 10 percent of chemistry questions have marks that require a *third read*—more than one-mark difference on a five-mark scale. While third-reader rates are less for lower-stream courses, where stakes for students are somewhat lower, these studies, replicated with similar results during every examination period over several years, reveal how difficult it is to achieve consistency.

Humans experience factors that expose their fallibilities. Their ability to concentrate is disrupted by fatigue, hunger, noise, and emotional distractions in their lives. Technology is advancing to the degree that computers can be "trained" to mark papers without experiencing any of these distractors, and they can mark around the clock while humans sleep.

Our region conducted numerous studies comparing computer and teacher marks with amazing results. A recent study reported by Andrea Sands in the May 23, 2014, issue of the *Calgary Herald* stated that "A computer could do a better job than a teacher in marking grade 12 diploma exam essays. . . . [One company's] automated algorithms outperformed human reliability in the study by about 20 percent." Perhaps the move to automated vehicles will be the impetus to trust technology when marking students' tests.

Technology is already used routinely to replace humans in marking short-answer questions on tests; yet automating the marking of students' *essay answers* may be too controversial for some. For this reason, school systems using technology resort to a two-marker approach, where one is a teacher and the other a computer program. A third teacher provides the additional read when the first two markings reveal a discrepancy. In the final analysis, *providing a fair mark to students is what really matters even though technology is involved.*

Conspicuous by its absence in educational research is evidence that there is consistency in teachers' assessments. Educators and their unions are unable to counter concerns regarding assessment inconsistencies. Until there is evidence that students' work is measured accurately and consistently across the educational system, trust requires a *check-and-balance* approach such as is provided through *large-scale standardized assessment accompanied by anonymous marking*. Teacher unions need to abandon their self-serving agenda in favor of fairness to students. Politicians need to support students rather than pander to unions.

Teacher-preparation programs are not ameliorating the problem. Our surveys of teacher preparedness showed that new teachers indicate preparedness for assessing student work as their greatest concern. Once these teachers enter the school system, they are confronted with their weaknesses. In regions not using standardized testing, there is less likelihood that teacher marks face a sustained challenge from parents. The advent of standardized testing has altered the landscape, and now significant sums of taxpayer funding to school districts is designated toward teacher in-service on assessment. The problem is complex, however, and inconsistency remains.

ASSESSMENT INCONSISTENCY AND GRADE INFLATION

As already stated, teachers bring their biases to the assessment process. Inconsistency in assessment is the central issue, but it is exacerbated by a tendency toward grade inflation. We can identify it as *inflation* because classroom marks assigned by teachers are *skewed upward rather than in both directions*. Teacher bias toward inflation likely stems from their belief that content was taught; the teacher then assumes more from the student's answer than what should be credited. In other words, the teacher believes what is taught is caught. So pervasive is this assumption that one superintendent opined that grade inflation in his district was not endemic, it was pandemic.

The Organisation for Economic Co-operation and Development, which administers the triannual PISA test, published a report in 2012 that discussed grade inflation in the United States. It concluded that, "While anecdotal evidence on grade inflation abounds, studies on grade inflation in secondary schools are scarce. The existing evidence signals that grade inflation is common and that, at least in the United States, it has been increasing since the 1990s" (p. 2).

This report raises the matter of the *paucity of research on grade inflation in secondary schools*. Avoiding unpleasant research about the school system is the natural disposition within a school system, and reinforcing a message that classroom teachers are adherents to low standards is troublesome to taxpayers, especially when their funding to education is already one of the highest in the world, as is the case with the United States. Administrators and their political overseers are loath to disclose information that might be embarrassing, especially when other regions nearby are maintaining secrecy.

Problems emanating from inconsistent marking can also be somewhat muted when marks are raised and parents get an unwarranted rosy picture of their child's academic progress. When messages sent home reflect high standing, everyone is happy. More importantly, there are no complaints. *The result is that standards decline until something—such as standardized-test results—happens to challenge the marking system.* For this reason, parents should give special attention to standardized-test results and request that these results be made available to them whenever reviewing their child's academic progress.

In the United Kingdom, a Durham University study concluded that an A grade awarded in 2009 was the equivalent to a C grade awarded in the 1980s. According to *The Telegraph*, this shocking trend goes hand-in-hand with the "all must have prizes" ethos that has dominated education for decades, to the detriment of academic excellence. The newspaper's summative statement was that these effects of grade inflation have become "endemic" in public examinations (2009).

Whether it is endemic as suggested by the newspaper or pandemic as suggested by the superintendent, grade inflation is a serious problem because it is *fraudulent*. Thomas and Bainbridge (1997) examined many school districts in the United States and demonstrated how an inconsistent application in standards produces *unfairness*. In figure 7.1, students from school A received the lowest marks of the five schools on the SAT as well as on norm referenced tests in reading and math. Nevertheless, students received high marks from their teachers and received a collective grade point average of 3.6.

In school E, students scored the highest of the five schools on the external tests but had the lowest grade point average. These authors summarized their overall findings:

> It is extremely difficult to explain how the lowest achieving school can have a higher grade point average than the higher achieving schools. Yet this same pattern is found in most of the school districts in which the authors have conducted School Effectiveness Audits. . . . The conclusion can be drawn that in low achieving schools with high grade point averages, expectations are extremely low—just the opposite of what research indicates should be done. Having low expectations begets low achievement. The fraud is that the high-grade point average gives a false message to the students. Schools which expect little and provide high grades, regardless of the level of academic achievement, are fraudulent educational systems and should be corrected. (Thomas and Bainbridge, 1997)

This summative conclusion may sound harsh when the term *fraud* is used; however, when the public is led to believe something that is beyond misleading and actually false, how else should it be characterized? The report also reminds us that low achievement is the result of low expectations because

Educational Fraud

SCHOOL	SAT	Norm Referenced Test (%ile) Reading	Norm Referenced Test (%ile) Math	GRADE POINT
A	750	35	26	3.6
B	900	40	42	3.2
C	990	48	48	2.8
D	1050	58	55	2.6
E	1125	67	74	2.5

Figure 7.1. Comparing external test scores and grade point averages.

students are misled to believe they are doing well and additional study time is unnecessary.

In 2008, the *Queen's Journal* at Queens University in Ontario demonstrated the extent of grade inflation throughout an entire province (Woods, 2008). Faced with increasing numbers of students seeking entry to a limited number of postsecondary placements, teachers endeavored to give their students an advantage in qualifying for entry by lowering their standards.

McGill University acknowledged that students from Ontario were going to have their grades *deflated* by 7 percent to achieve greater fairness for students applying from other provinces. Ontario's abolition of province-wide exams decades earlier meant that the teacher's mark was the final mark; students registering with an A grade had increased from 18 percent in 1992 to 40 percent in 2007. The *Queen's Journal* editorial concluded that "the number of A-students isn't growing because people are getting smarter. Rather, academic standards have declined so it is easier to get an A than ever before—a phenomenon known as grade inflation" (Woods, 2008).

James Côté, sociology professor at the University of Western Ontario, writes that

> Grade inflation creates an education system that hurts students. It differentiates among students less and gives them less feedback on the quality of work. It's generally a disincentive for working harder because it really means it's easier to get a higher grade. For the students who deserve the higher grade in the first place it can be demoralizing . . . It also gives people false feedback that they themselves are above average. They get an inflated view of themselves in terms of who they are and what they can do academically. (Côté, 2009, n.p.)

Côté continues, "Standardized testing would help curb the problem. . . . We're hesitant to [use standardized tests] in Canada, but it would help" (n.p.).

Of course, standardized tests would help! Côté and Anton (2007) summarize their assessment of the issue:

> In 2007, 40 percent of Ontario high school graduates leave with A averages— 8 times as many as would be awarded in the traditional British system. In Alberta, as of 2007, just over 20 percent of high school graduates leave with an A average. This discrepancy may be explained by the fact that all Alberta high school students must write province-wide standardized exams, Diploma exams, in core subjects, in order to graduate. (n.p.)

Alberta is the only one of these five provinces that mandates diploma examinations. *Using provincial examinations, Alberta's educational system is able to limit the amount of grade inflation in its schools.* There still is evidence that grade inflation occurs and that it is significant, but the check-and-balance approach provide for greater accuracy and consistency in assessing student work.

This University of Saskatchewan study "also confirms what many of us in admissions suspected or knew anecdotally—grade inflation is common and the best students come from Alberta high schools" (Millington, 2011). McClure (2011), a reporter from the *Calgary Herald* reported on this study and Dr. McQuillan, the University of Calgary's dean of Arts, who said, "As admissions become more difficult and competitive, each school in Ontario tends to say let's give our students a leg up by giving them higher grades. . . . There's an arms race of A's going on."

While Ontario universities were loath to admit it publicly for fear of creating controversy, registrars told McQuillan that they were *quietly adjusting the marks for Alberta students to compensate*. A follow-up in the *Vancouver Sun* reported that the University of British Columbia "adds two percentage points to the averages of students applying from Alberta because the grading system is tougher in that province" (Steffenhagen, 2012). The piece quoted Michael Bluhm, UBC's associate director of undergraduate admissions, as saying,

> We recognize this difference when evaluating Alberta students for admission. I'll be clear to state that this is not a boost or benefit, per se, to Alberta students over BC students; rather it is an acknowledgment that the two grading systems are different. Alberta is the only province where we currently see valid and quantifiable data to warrant consideration in our admission decisions.

Alberta is the only province with a complete regimen of school-leaving examinations, which provides evidence of how standardized testing provides some control over teachers' propensity to lower standards in their classroom assessments.

While Alberta's students experienced less grade inflation than students from other provinces, grade inflation still is evident in their high schools. Figure 7.2 demonstrates an interesting phenomenon. First, the general portrayal in this chart *is replicated annually and in all subjects* where there are two course streams. In this case, Social Studies 30 is the upper-stream course leading to a university program, and the data demonstrate consistently that the school marks from teachers are higher than the Diploma Examination marks for both the acceptable standard or passing, and the standard of excellence, or an A grade.

For example, in the first year, as indicated at the figure's left edge, 14 percent more students achieved the *acceptable standard* and 40 percent more achieved the *standard of excellence* from their school than there were students in that year who earned those marks on the Diploma Examination. This pattern of high discrepancies of numbers of students achieving a standard of

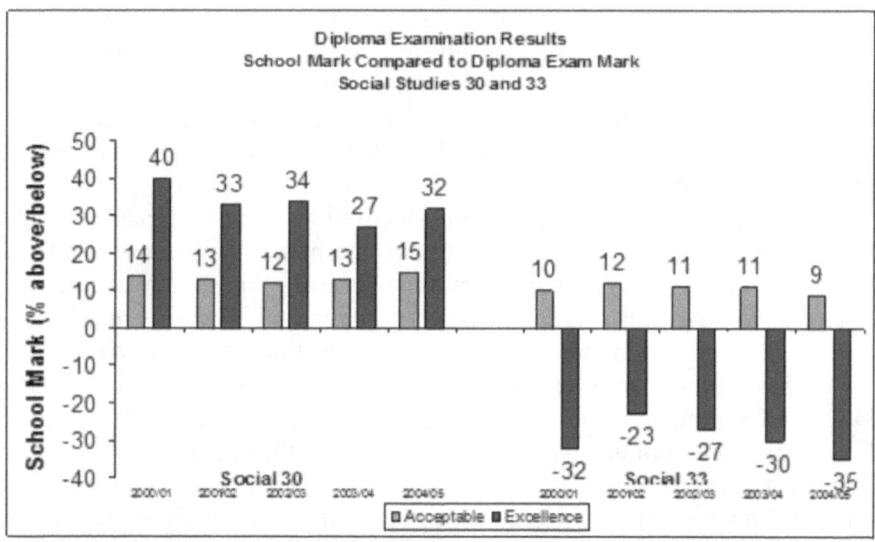

Figure 7.2. Diploma examination marks for social studies.

excellence is a second key aspect and is important because it is at this standard that scholarships are won and placements in prestigious universities are achieved. Stakes are highest at the for students achieving the standard of excellence. The consistency of this discrepancy evident across the years is amazing.

Equally noteworthy is the pattern on the right-hand side of the figure for the *lower-stream* Social Studies 33. Again, the variances between school-generated marks and Diploma Examination scores are consistent from year to year. There is, however, a strange pattern for the standard of excellence, because Diploma Examination marks are substantially below school-generated marks. The explanation comes from interactions with many teachers of the lower-stream courses who have indicated that they do *not give out A marks in lower-stream courses because the student chose the easier stream.*

Teachers believe that students avoided the challenge of taking the more difficult stream. Therefore teachers exercised their own *bias* in assessing student achievement by *penalizing* them for taking the easier course. In effect, *teachers disregarded course standards and applied their own.* Not only were these trends evident in social studies classes, but they were also replicated in mathematics, English, and science classes. Inaccurate student assessments in classrooms are biased toward inflation except when there is a perceived need to penalize students for not taking on coursework the teachers believe to be more challenging.

In a provincial meeting of school-board trustees, an ex-teacher of Social Studies 33 took the podium and reiterated this *penalty* aspect to her colleagues. She openly acknowledged never giving an A to students because she felt that students should have registered for the more challenging Social Studies 30 course. Even though her students had responded to examination questions at the A level, she imposed her biases on students by penalizing their choice in subjects.

A final aspect of this Alberta study focused on what took place in each school district across the province. Again, the pattern was consistent from year to year, with only minor exceptions. Basically, in all school districts, *school-generated marks in upper-stream courses were higher than Diploma Examination marks*. If this trend was not indicating grade inflation there, would have been a *relatively equal number of districts above and below*. Diploma Examinations may provide a check and balance for grade inflation, but elimination is not guaranteed; rather, it reduces the potential.

One Alberta parent, upon reviewing these disturbing studies, commented on how important it is not only to ensure consistent standards across the country *but around the world as well*. She understood that registrars across Canada were adjusting student applicants according to province, but what about students applying for placements in other countries? Her child had applied to Harvard but had not been accepted. Defending fairness in an environment where students' marks are highly inflated is difficult, because the degree of grade inflation is grossly unequal. There are winners and losers, and teachers' sense of pride increases when their students are the winners.

Alberta's success at maintaining standards resulted in the parent's child receiving a more accurate set of marks, but this otherwise commendable state of affairs may have penalized her child, and presumably many others, who would otherwise have been accepted into a prestigious university in another country unfamiliar with the high standards in one Canadian province. For this reason, universities must be cognizant of student achievement whenever international testing, such as PISA, occurs so that they adjust acceptance standards as demonstrated by McGill University.

The interconnectedness of these studies on grade inflation within the educational system demonstrates the concern in Canada regarding fairness to students seeking entry into postsecondary institutions. A student should qualify for scholarships and gain entry to prestigious universities because of *merit based on achievement rather than luck based on location of residence*.

GRADE INFLATION LEADS TO LOWER LEVELS OF STUDENT ACHIEVEMENT

Disadvantaging worthy students is not the only unfairness that results from grade inflation, as Thomas and Bainbridge's earlier-referenced study points out. The authors found that students who received high grade point averages in their study of six schools had lower scores on the SAT and standardized tests. Where grade inflation was the greatest, actual student achievement as measured by standardized assessments was the lowest.

Laurie (2007) undertook a similar study in Canada's Maritime Provinces, located across the U.S. border from New England. His finding, subsequently replicated in regional research, found that in schools where students received marks most above their Diploma Examination scores, the examination scores were relatively the lowest in the test group. The opposite was also true: in schools where students experienced the least grade inflation, the students had the relatively highest examination scores.

Students who receive inflated marks from their schools do not demonstrate similarly high levels of achievement on exit examinations because *they suffer from a false sense of security*. They mistakenly believe they are doing well in the course. Schools that expect little and provide high grades, regardless of the level of academic achievement, are purveyors of a fraudulent education that leaves parents and children believing something that is not true. Such action is unconscionable and should be exposed, confronted, and corrected.

One superintendent expressed her difficulty in adequately responding to a group of graduating students who had received high marks from their schools but significantly lower marks on their final examinations. The universities to which these students had applied had advised the students that they would only be provisionally accepted because the combined score from the exams and the schools was too low. Dreams were shattered and the superintendent—the visible scapegoat—became the object of an outpouring of anger.

This pattern of grade inflation was evident year after year for many students in the same grade 12 class at that school. Students were lulled into apathy or, even worse, into self-aggrandizement, thinking that, even in cases when they had not performed academically, they had aced the course; consequently, they were not diligent about preparing for the standardized test. In this specific instance, the superintendent had the uncomfortable task of saying that nothing could be done for the students except for them to retake the course the next year to better master the material they had clearly not learned.

This unfortunate incident illustrates the general inability of teachers to grade student achievement in an objective and accurate manner. Webber et al. (2009) summarized their interviews with secondary school principals by stating that, "secondary principals were not very positive about teacher knowledge and practice in matters of fairness and equity and assessment." Yet stakes are high in secondary schools where scholarships are won and entrances to prestigious universities are granted.

TEACHERS GRADUATE FROM A SYSTEM PLAGUED BY GRADE INFLATION

Educators may excuse this tendency to inflate grades by pointing out that grade inflation is rampant in universities as well. Teachers come out of an education system where marks below B are seldom awarded and where failure is virtually nonexistent. Koedel (2011) analyzed major academic departments at universities and reported how education marks are skewed upward. *Grade point averages for students enrolled in a school's department of education were much higher than they were in any other department.*

Koedel and colleagues found that

> Students who take education classes at universities receive significantly higher grades than students who take classes in every other academic discipline. The higher grades cannot be explained by observable differences in student quality between education majors and other students, nor can they be explained by the fact that education classes are typically smaller than classes in other academic departments. The remaining reasonable explanation is that the higher grades in education classes are the result of low grading standards. These low grading standards likely will negatively affect the accumulation of skills for prospective teachers during university training. More generally, they contribute to a larger culture of low standards for educators. . . . While all other university departments work in one space, education departments work in another. . . . The data consistently show that education departments award exceptionally favorable grades to virtually all their students in all their classes.

Babcock (2010) indicates that *grade inflation is associated with reduced student effort* in college: put simply, students in classes where it is easier to get an A do not work as hard. He demonstrated that in classes where the expected *grade point average* rises by one point, students respond by reducing effort, as measured by study time, *by at least 20 percent*. The implication for education, therefore, is that *teachers who are being trained know less because their marks are so high.*

Koedel estimated that, "If the grading standards in each education department were moved to align with the average grading standards at their respective universities, student effort would rise by at least 11 to 14 percent." Koedel proceeded to provide a hypothesis regarding why education departments having these deplorably skewed results escape detection:

One notable difference between education departments and other major departments at universities is that virtually all graduates from education departments move into a single sector of the labor market—education. If the education sector is less effective at identifying low-quality graduates than are other sectors of the labor market, this would help explain why professors in education departments are able to consistently award As to most students. (Koedel, 2009)

Most university departments serve a diverse market. For example, a school's business department seeks to place graduates in an array of firms that can easily discern the differences in the quality of graduates among multiple institutions. *Firms would cease hiring from lower-quality programs, forcing instructors to recalibrate their standards.* Education, on the other hand, is a closed system. Graduates are generally employed locally by the school board, which participates in the fostering of a culture of low standards. Like a university's department of education, the local school district is reticent to distinguish good teachers from mediocre teachers.

We have also pointed out that accountability in postsecondary education is out of balance and skewed because it relies on student-satisfaction surveys. Over time, academic grades for work of comparable quality have increased in what is known as the *standards creep*. It appears that the faculties of education also suffer from a severe case of having low expectations from their students who, eventually, work with our children, preparing them for the real world.

GRADE INFLATION IS HIGHEST FOR THE HIGHER ACHIEVERS

Christina Wall (2003) proposed another reason for rampant grade inflation, following her investigation into the subject, concluding that "grade inflation is prominent in most schools today. Perhaps it is due to the emphasis on morale. It could also be due to the emphasis of having good grades in order to get into good colleges and become successful." Wall's research and conclusion is generalizable throughout the literature but requires that we consider *why it occurs in elementary and middle school as well*. Students at these grade levels do not need a leg up to gain entry into some prestigious university program.

In the regional study Wall undertook, students wrote system-wide tests in grades 3, 6, and 9. These were low-stakes tests, and teachers were encouraged to mark their students' written responses as a first read or as a preliminary reading before the school forwarded the tests to a marking center *where anonymity was ensured*. This process enabled the province to study the impact a teacher-student relationship had on the grade a student received. *Spe-*

cifically, the student's teacher and an anonymous teacher marked the same piece of work, and we could determine whether there were differences and, if so, what the trend might be.

The first phase of this study took five years and demonstrated a consistent result for each year and at each grade of the tests. At the acceptable standard, up to 8 percent more students achieved a pass from their classroom teacher than from the anonymous marker. At the standard of excellence, 86 percent more students received an A-level mark from their classroom teacher than from the anonymous marker. Because grade inflation in the classroom was so dramatic at the upper achievement levels, a meeting with superintendents was held to discuss the problem.

Superintendents were loath to undertake any action to ameliorate the problem. Large-scale testing was a contentious proposition, and acknowledging these significantly different results in marks was thought to be inflammatory and likely lead to a backlash from union members, which at that time included principals. In the five years that followed, 79 percent more students still received the standard of excellence mark from their classroom teacher than from the marking center where student anonymity was tightly controlled. *Teachers' inconsistent marking is a problem made more worrisome from their tendency to inflate student scores, especially scores at the upper levels.*

Unfortunately, grade inflation, which unfairly disadvantages and advantages students, is not the only malevolent feature in the marking process. Subjectivity can seriously distort academic achievement as demonstrated by the triennial Canadian national testing program—the PCAP, or the Pan-Canadian Assessment Program. This program includes extensive surveying that provides a context in which we can assess the nature of various relationships associated with student achievement.

One question on the PCAP asked teachers whether they incorporate *improvement* over a period of time when they assign letter grades related to achievement. In other words, were students' final marks indicating how well they could divide influenced by how much they improved from the beginning of the term? Teachers who responded affirmatively in the different provinces ranged from 13 percent to 72 percent. A second year, but with a different subject and different teachers responding to the same question, indicated a range of 13 percent to 66 percent. These variations demonstrate how assessments of student achievement vary across provinces yet are consistent across teaching, regardless of subject.

Another question focused on *attendance* and asked whether students' marks were influenced by this issue. Presumably students were penalized with lower marks if they were absent an inordinate number of days. On this issue, teachers from various jurisdictions varied in their response, from 6 percent to 66 percent. As with the previous question, these high and low responses were not significant outliers. In other words, other jurisdictions were spread out across the range with several relatively near to both ends of the scale.

Teachers also indicated as to whether or not their assessment of the student was influenced by his or her *participation* during class activities. Participation is a desired student behavior, but is it indicative of student learning in curriculum outcomes? Once again teachers varied widely in their attitudes, with as few as 12 percent saying they would in some districts and as many as 63 percent saying they would in others.

Improvement over time, attendance, and participation are all qualities associated with being a good student. Parents want to know how their child is doing in these areas because they are good predictors of how well their child will perform in the workplace. However, should these qualities be conflated into an index of what constitutes a good student when the grade is intended to measure *competency* in a skill or mastery of a concept? Logic suggests that it would be more truthful and more helpful if these valuable qualities were assessed independently and reported elsewhere.

The confusion on this issue opens the door to *inconsistency in assessment* and, therefore, *unfairness toward a segment of the student population.* If these or any other criteria such as behavior, status in the class, cleanliness or neatness is considered when reporting achievement in a subject, teacher bias is introduced.

INCORPORATING NONACADEMIC FACTORS INTO ACHIEVEMENT REDUCES SUCCESS

For these nonacademic factors, it is noteworthy that of all the Canadian provinces, Alberta was at the lowest end of the scale on three of the questions surveyed (including the two years when improvement had been the focus) and within 3 percent from the bottom on the fourth. Yet this province persistently recorded the *lowest percentage of teacher assessments* for Canadian students with a mark of 70 percent or higher. In other words, *Alberta students had the lowest set of class marks from teachers across the entire country while having the lowest percentage of teachers conflating marks for learning with behavior.*

At the same time this province repeatedly scored the *highest* on national and international assessments. The applicable generalization is that the jurisdiction with the strictest adherence to marking relative to standards and the least likelihood of subjectivity leading to bias and grade inflation also had the highest levels of student achievement as measured on standardized tests.

Figure 7.3 demonstrates that on each criterion, students' test marks were significantly lower when the teacher included consideration of the criterion then when it was not considered.

For example, students with teachers who indicated they did not include *attendance* in their students' marks scored an average of 495 in their reading-achievement test. Students who had teachers who indicated they did include attendance scored some 30 points lower on the achievement test. In each instance, using a nonacademic factor yielded a lower result in this national assessment of reading.

It is apparent, therefore, that teachers who are prone to incorporating nonacademic criteria do their students a disservice, because including these biases leave students with an inflated understanding of their learning. They experience a disincentive to work harder. In simple language, *teachers are disadvantaging their students by not confining their marks to what their students learned.*

While Alberta's students benefitted from assessment based on standards, this benefit evaporated when the province's school boards began importing many teachers from the rest of Canada to accommodate a class-size-reduction program and the retirement of a significant number of teachers. The national testing program's survey registered an immediate change in the

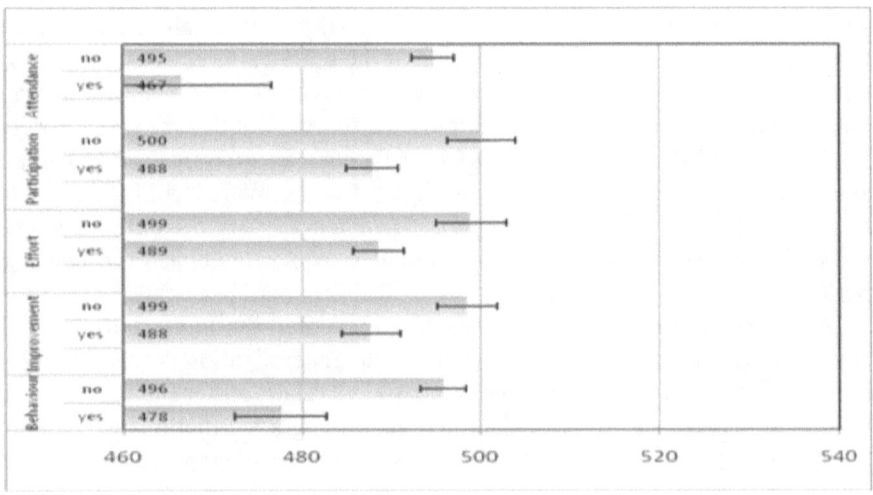

Figure 7.3. Examining specific nonacademic criteria in grading.

degree to which Alberta teachers utilized *nonacademic factors* in assigning final marks for their students.

Previous national studies routinely demonstrated that Alberta teachers were relatively averse to using nonacademic factors; with the influx of new teachers associated with increased population stemming from oil production, data ballooned to the point where 64 percent of Alberta's teachers indicated they were now employing such an approach to grading.

Webber et al. (2009) conducted a follow-up study in Alberta and determined that teachers always or often used factors such as:

- Penalties for late assignments (33 percent)
- Adjusted grades to recognize student behavior (17 percent)
- Adjusted grades to recognize neatness (11 percent)
- Adjusted grades based on student attendance (6 percent)
- And bonus marks for extra work (35 percent).

Their study went on to ask students whether they felt teachers assessed a variety of factors in addition to academic achievement when they were given a score in a subject. The results affirmed that this was the case. In their mind, grades were adjusted for the following reasons:

- Report-card marks were change because of late assignments (87 percent agreed)
- Grades were adjusted to recognize student behavior (47 percent of secondary and 70 percent of elementary agreed)
- Grades were adjusted because of how neat the work was (31 percent at secondary and 69 percent at elementary agreed)
- And bonus marks were awarded for extra work (48 percent agreed).

A summative statement from the researchers indicated that "secondary students admonished that the system is for teachers, not students, and that teacher bias is a real problem. Students who are favored get better marks. . . . Grades are reduced for misbehavior, and if a student is disruptive then grades go down" (Webber et al., 2009).

Concurrently a significant shift occurred in the province-wide Diploma Examination marks. We have already indicated that system-wide examination marks are always lower than school-generated marks. So predictable is this outcome that only rarely does any one of the 62 school districts record an average examination mark that is higher than that assigned by teachers. Despite the province's outstanding success on the world stage of international testing, there still was grade inflation, albeit to a lesser degree than in any other Canadian jurisdiction.

During a three-year period of extensive teacher hiring and turnover, grade inflation increased dramatically. At the beginning of this three-year period, only *three* districts had a variance greater than 10 percent between the average school and examination marks for English. Three years later, *17* districts *exceeded* the 10 percent threshold; this occurred even though *provincial examination marks* demonstrated a *significant decline*.

In mathematics, this threshold was *exceeded* by only *five* districts at the beginning of the study but increased to *eighteen* by the conclusion of the study made in Webber et al. (2009). The significant increase in school-generated marks was not matched by a similar gain in learning on the provincial exit examination. In the initial year of this study, 83 percent of students met the examination's acceptable standard; three years later it remained essentially the same (82 percent).

The same was true with the highest level, known as the standard of excellence: over the three-year period, the decline was inconsequential. Since these exams are now set to be equal in difficulty from year to year, all that changed was the teacher-generated mark, which increased significantly and reflected a new interpretation of the standards.

During this period, another disturbing story emerged from surveys of employers that the province conducted. Employer satisfaction with graduates' skills and quality of work plummeted to their lowest level, with a decline from 77 percent satisfaction to 67 percent. Such a dramatic decline had never occurred before, which raised concerns about a growing mismatch between teachers' ability to assess students' achievement and employers' need to have skilled workers. This variation between classroom marks and employer perceptions provided another indication that grade inflation within the classroom was increasing.

Introducing nonacademic factors into the assessments of student achievement produced significant grade inflation at a time when national and international assessments indicated achievement was declining. Meanwhile class-size reduction, which was purported to improve the learning environment, required the province to increase the number of teachers by 13 percent. Growth in enrollment and a wave or retirements associated with an aging workforce also drove up the number of hires, many of whom were unfamiliar with the province's curricular standards. These factors coalesced to create a negative impact on achievement.

A SIMPLE ILLUSTRATION OF HOW GRADE INFLATION OCCURS

One more point needs to be made. The longitudinal data reveals how insidious grade inflation can be. Both the examination and school marks were based on percentages, and school marks were skewed significantly to the right. Because student test scores produced a normal distribution, we can be confident that test developers successfully differentiated students based on achievement.

School-generated marks, however, did not demonstrate a normal distribution, which means factors other than student achievement were in play. For example, in one course required for university entrance, more than three times as many students received a mark of 80 percent as did those recorded in the examination. At 90 percent, it was double, and school marks were significantly skewed upward beginning at 70 percent. There was another curious fact that strongly suggests the presence of human bias and predilection.

In our modern economy, we often round up or down in an effort to make things simpler. In teacher-recorded marks, the study revealed a very discernible pattern of rounding up that would have had nothing to do with achievement. For example, there were many scores that ended in zeroes or fives—far more than would have been statistically expected. At the same time, there were disproportionately few grades recorded as X8, or X9.

Schools were systematically *bumping up marks* by one or two percentages to qualify for a higher letter grade or scholarship. The rounding up was not compensated with a rounding down, and while this explains a minor portion of how grade inflation occurs, the story does not end here. Because the bump-ups are not universally applied, so that fewer students received a mark ending in eight or nine, we can assume that that some teachers and some schools took a different approach to assessment. In other words, some teachers did not round up marks for students with grade percentages ending in X8 or X9.

Students in the rounding-up schools temporarily benefitted, but others did not. To what do we attribute this fundamental unfairness: Gender? Compliant behavior? This question will be discussed, in part, later. The point here is that a pattern of unfairness exists in the system and that the evidence extends across all subjects and over many years. Application of certain biases was routinely practiced at the school level and contributed to the natural inclination toward grade inflation. Lower standards at the school level were the norm.

STUDENT CHEATING AND GRADE INFLATION

It is possible that concerns with grade inflation at the school level are compounded by a disconcerting problem that is frequently overlooked and often not even acknowledged. Cheating can profoundly inflate a student's grade, but it could be essentially eliminated on achievement tests if the school were to follow prescribed protocols. Perhaps this issue is too disconcerting for educators to even acknowledge. If factual, student cheating can seriously jeopardize student fairness.

Academic cheating in postsecondary institutions is well documented. This is less so for the K–12 system, although what we do know is equally disturbing. McCabe, Treviño, and Butterfield (2001) studied high school cheating involving 4,500 U.S. schools and found that:

- 74 percent of students admitted to serious test cheating
- 72 percent admitted to serious cheating on written work
- 97 percent admitted to copying homework or to test copying
- 30 percent admitted to repetitive, serious cheating on tests and exams
- 15 percent had obtained a term paper from the Internet
- And 52 percent had copied a few sentences from a website without citing the source.

Unfortunately, the *2002 Report Card on the Ethics of American Youth* (Josephson Institute of Ethics, 2002) determined that cheating was *on the rise*. Comparing their student survey results for 1992 and 2002, the percentage of students admitting that they had cheated on an examination increased from 61 percent to 74 percent.

Newberger (1999) compared data with that from the 1940s and found that in a 1997 survey of high achievers in high school, 87 percent judged cheating to be "common" among their peers. Seventy-six percent confessed they themselves had cheated. By way of contrast, a national sample of U.S. college students in the 1940s found that only 20 percent admitted to cheating in high school *when they were questioned anonymously*. Cheating is considerably more prevalent today, and contrary to some people's opinion, *cheating is not restricted to weak students attempting to improve their chances at passing.*

Niels (2014) researched the major reasons why students cheat and published his results online on the website About.com (January 17, 2014.) His research led him to believe that students cheated for the following reasons:

1. There is a mechanism within each of us that triggers a need to save face. Saving face can mean a desire to save oneself from the angry assault of a parent or teacher.
2. Cheating is no longer deviant behavior but normal behavior because everybody does it.
3. Cheating offers an easy way out. Why bother studying hard and doing all those term papers by yourself if you can use someone else's work?

Niels's findings support the notion that cheating can occur with students of *every ability level whenever they see the need to get ahead without expending the necessary effort*. These findings also imply that the odds of being caught are relatively low.

Newberger (1999) also verifies that the odds of getting away with academic cheating are heavily in the cheater's favor. "Ninety per cent of the confessed cheaters surveyed by *Who's Who* said they had never been caught. . . . The incentive has changed from passing by the weak student to getting into select universities by the stronger students" (n.p.).

In the regional study, cheating on standardized, system-wide tests, where the process occurs under tight security, was very low, with an incidence rate of 1 percent whenever two or more students were detected as having the same pattern of answers. Invigilators systematically monitored the examination room; furthermore, students writing the same test were surrounded with open space and could be observed from multiple angles.

It is noteworthy that in the few instances when students did cheat, *they were writing tests they deemed to be of the greatest importance.* This included tests in subjects that were required for a graduation diploma and entrance into university. In other words, these students were the stronger ones wishing to retain their place in the system that would eventually allow entrance into prestigious university programs and a future path to a well-paying job.

The reality of stronger students cheating to succeed in a competitive environment was corroborated by Davis, Drinan, and Gallant (2009):

> It's not the dumb kids who cheat . . . it's the kids with a 4.6 grade point average who are under such pressure to keep their grades up and get into the best colleges. They're the ones who figure out how to cheat without getting caught. . . . Grades are a commodity in our knowledge society, and, with many students, they represent the end goal of schooling.

The goal of saving face in an environment that increasingly appears to view cheating as normal is observable in the lower grades. Bushway and Nash (1977) indicated that even as of several decades ago "academic dishonesty is endemic in all levels of education. In the United States, studies show that 20 percent of students started cheating in the first grade." Similarly, other U.S. studies reveal that 56 percent of middle school students admit to cheating (Decoo, 2002).

Canadian researchers have not given as much attention to cheating as those in the United States. Nevertheless, the work that has been done reveals a pattern like that found in the United States. In 2006, the University of Guelph and Rutgers University surveyed 15,000 students and found that "73 percent of university students reported instances of serious cheating on written work while in high school" (Ho, 2012).

The discussion on cheating has focused, thus far, on student behavior that is covert. There also is an overt form of cheating that perhaps may not be referred to as *cheating* because it is an encouraged activity. Davis et al. (2009) describes this activity that ends up giving some students an advantage over their peers. "Think of a student who receives 'help' from his parents on his science project or her essay. If a student is transparent about the assistance received, she might not receive as high a grade [as] if the teacher thinks the student did her assignment on her own." How frequently does this type of advantage occur?

Canada's PCAP national testing program asked thirteen-year-old students across the nation how frequently they worked with parents on their homework. Two out of three students affirmed that they received assistance: 35 percent said it occurred a few times a month, 26 percent said it happened a few times a week, and 6 percent said that it happened almost daily. We likely experience some inner turmoil with any suggestion that this parental assistance is cheating; yet if the teacher is not aware of it and is assessing the product in any way, some students are advantaged. Some are then disadvantaged. *Unfairness has occurred.*

These surveys also asked teachers to identify how frequently homework assignments were used in determining marks. Given that 44 percent indicated that assignments were used to determine the final mark, it is apparent that some students were clearly advantaged and that the advantage was a significant factor. Hopefully teachers are sufficiently astute to track the degree to which their students receive assistance. To the degree this monitoring does not occur, we can assume that grade inflation is translating as unfairness to students. Ryan (1998) references unfairness resulting from plagiarism that is equally applicable to any unknown assistance.

> Often lost in the discussion of plagiarism is the interest of the students who don't cheat. They do legitimate research and write their own papers. They work harder (and learn more) than the plagiarists, yet their grades may suffer when their papers are judged and graded against papers that are superior but stolen material. Students have a right to expect fairness in the classroom. When teachers turn a blind eye to plagiarism, it undermines that right and denigrates grades, degrees, and even institutions.

Many teachers and administrators understand how grade inflation occurs because they receive students into their programs who struggle to learn yet receive relatively high grades. Research evidence indicates that assessment of student achievement is inconsistent because various forms of bias find their way into a teacher's mind-set. As offensive as the thought of any unfairness to students might be with some, anytime students are advantaged or disadvantaged by these biases, the result is *unfair to some or all*. There is no merit in attempting to cloak the issue in secrecy as so frequently occurs.

This issue of fairness has a parallel in professional golf. In that game, each player is responsible to monitor and, if necessary, challenge the decisions of competitors playing in the same group. The winner of a golf tournament is the player with the lowest score over several rounds. Because there are many groups of players and insufficient numbers of referees to observe each golfer, players are responsible to their fellow competitors in other groups to ensure that a competitor in their group is scoring by the rules. This practice is a check and balance for ensuring fairness for the field of golfers in the tournament. Golf may be an honorable sport, but trust has its limitations.

A focus in education should be about *trust versus accountability*. Teachers want parents and the public to trust unquestioningly their assessments of student learning. Their unions understand that without large-scale testing the entire accountability effort in the K–12 system collapses. Such an environment is like what exists in most postsecondary programs where instructors hide behind "academic freedom" to avoid accountability.

Sole discretion to determine the curriculum and the assessment of learning is the preferred situation for teacher unions, which argue that every learning environment is unique and that therefore nothing is in common and capable of standardization. This leaves the classroom an impregnable fortress in which the teacher—namely, the lord of the domain—rules benevolently without fear of accountability.

It is a state of affairs that could not and will not survive. Public scrutiny today, born in part out of a growing awareness of the conclusions researchers are drawing from multiple longitudinal studies, makes it clear that the old way must go. Trust will remain but in a new and open context in which respectful dialogue and a new attitude of cliental service emerges.

The global community is altering the K–12 system because the advent of standardized testing now identifies which countries are providing higher levels of student learning. Results from these cyclical tests are like the sports environment, where athletes come together every four years for athletic contests. In education, these tests are like an Olympics of Learning, with one significant variation: Rather than involving the elite athletes, as in sport, random samples of the general student population are involved in measuring education. The focus, therefore, is on the average.

As in sport, where countries undertake initiatives to improve athletic performance, and thereby raise the bar of excellence for themselves and others, educational leaders today also feel pressure to stay abreast of rising international standards. Strategies for improvement may be in the form of increased resources or accountability. The result is that politics more than ever before are involved with education, and when this occurs, politicians inevitably choose sides.

A message of this chapter is that fairness to students requires a check-and-balance approach that features large-scale testing of student achievement with regard to established standards. The results leave students and their parents with an ability to judge for themselves how well the student is learning and to be confident that the measurement is a fair and accurate assessment of what it purports to measure.

This, in turn, creates the possibility of holding accountable those who are responsible for the learning environment. It is this measurement process that applies pressure on those within the educational system to improve their performance. *Reaction against this pressure is what produces the conflict that is now so evident in the politics of education.*

Teacher unions need to reexamine their resistance to large-scale testing. The evidence of the teacher's inability to assess student achievement in a consistent and fair manner is overwhelming. To be fair to students, unions must become advocates of a new approach that puts the best interest of students first while trusting that the welfare of teachers will be appropriately addressed. *As it now stands, unions are the significant inhibitors of fairness to students.*

Politicians faced with this conflict must consider their potential to win the next electoral contest. Will they side with the unions, who can readily influence their members' votes? Will they side with students, who have limited understanding of fairness issues and cannot vote? To what extent will they release information to the public so that they are more informed about the nature of the conflict? These are significant issues in educational politics, and it is necessary to draw politicians into the discussion so that their positions are clearly stated and publicly understood.

While we trust our service providers, it is folly to do it so blindly. As Edward Deming once put it, in God we trust; all others bring data. The data story in student assessment should provide our elected representatives with the evidence they need to take a public, persuasive stand that makes fairness to students the highest priority in their education platform.

Grade inflation is so dominant in our school system yet remains one of its best-kept secrets. School, district, and state and provincial administrators have an obligation to minimize such unfairness to students. Principals can reduce grade inflation by conducting discussions about grade level of achievement, referenced earlier, and by comparing teachers' classroom assessments for their students with results on standardized assessments.

In turn, district leadership can model their commitment by reviewing students' classroom marks in schools with those generated from standardized tests. Not only do these discussions increase principals' awareness of their expectation to monitor this insidious educational malady, they also remind the school system about the ongoing need for standardized testing. These reviews vigorously undertaken reinforce an important message that accountability is an investment rather than expense.

Finally, while the strategy referenced above is sensible because it introduces greater fairness to students, a similar review as required of principals and superintendents is expected of state and provincial administrators. Our experience is that these conversations seldom occur throughout school districts unless system leaders kick-start and then maintain the discussions. Holding leaders accountable generates some stress and resentment; however, someone must uphold the primacy of students.

Therefore, a requirement that each level of the school district present their school's or district's results to councils of students and parents is an important piece of this puzzle. These discussions with our clients produced an ongoing focus on a problem that required constant review. Providing this critical information to them ensured their support for ongoing accountability with classroom assessment despite educators' efforts to eliminate standardized testing and rid the system of its efforts to ensure fairness to students.

This chapter details the critical role each administrator must fulfill as well as the narrative supporting this responsibility. Our experience revealed schools' and districts' hesitance to reveal data out of fear that it would create conflict; to them, cherry-picking good news is preferable to demonstrating full transparency. Therefore, the preceding narrative can be used as evidence for conducting a regional review as well as provide examples of where to focus proactive attention.

The key points made in this chapter are that

- Teacher unions attempt to equate standardized testing with a lack of trust in their capacity to accurately assess student work
- "What we do for students we should do for teachers" is a key leadership principle
- Transparency is a new reality for teachers
- Research verifies that teachers' marks are a very unreliable means of measurement
- The bell-curve philosophy regarding quotas emerged because of inconsistent marking
- Assessment inconsistency is skewed toward grade inflation, which leads to fraudulent marks
- Grade inflation produces complacency and lower results on students' end-of-year course examinations
- Teachers' tendency to inflate student grades may stem from teacher-preparation programs, which produce highly inflated marks
- Grade inflation is greatest at the high end of mark distributions
- When nonacademic factors are incorporated into a student's achievement mark, there is less likelihood of academic success

- Grade inflation readily occurs in a percentage grading system because teachers routinely bump up marks to a number ending in 5 or 0
- And grade inflation also occurs because of increased levels of student cheating, which occurs more frequently at the higher levels of achievement.

Chapter Eight

Grade Inflation Is Not Uniformly Evident

Grade inflation, because of low standards in our classrooms, is documented in the previous chapter, and this problem is virtually universal across North America. *Numbers don't lie*, and the news should be more than disconcerting: *it should be distressing*. There is no value to our society by giving *undeserved* credit to students or by *defrauding* taxpayers, the clients of our school system, of the full value of their tax dollars. The greatest harm is perpetuated in our workforce, which *is developing a mind-set that maximum effort is not necessary.*

Inconsistent classroom assessment of students' academic achievement is a long-standing problem too frequently disregarded because the information is not transparently presented for public scrutiny. While this lack of transparency is an issue, inflated marks are seldom disputed by students or their parents, especially when the pattern shows that these high marks are not irregular blips but an ongoing problem throughout the school system.

This evidence about low standards in classrooms demonstrates how inconsistent teachers are when assessing their students' achievement. This chapter's focus is answering the question about whether grade inflation is uniformly evident across students' experiences, *because when grades are weighted equally, the weighting can still be considered fair. Unfairness rears its head when consistency is lacking.* Is there, then, another inconsistency that must be monitored by administrators seeking to ensure fairness to students? Specifically, does grade inflation occur equally across all student populations? This chapter's focus is whether grade inflation *is gender-related.*

GENDER UNFAIRNESS IN BRITISH COLUMBIA

An analysis of the 2015 school year results for British Columbia makes it difficult to corroborate their conclusion that gender unfairness does not exist in the classroom. This jurisdiction masks the degree to which the problem exists by rolling up the higher marks by lumping C+, B, and A marks into one category. We examined the data, specifically looking at the high grades earned by female students on standardized tests versus those they earned in the classroom and found that female students consistently receive the grade advantage:

- English 10: The advantage (scoring C+, B, or A) accorded to female students on the *exam* is 13 percent but in *classrooms* is 18 percent or *plus 5 percentage points*.
- Math 10 (Precalc.): The advantage (scoring C+, B, or A) accorded to female students on the exam is 1 percent but in classrooms is 6 percent or *plus 5 percentage points*.
- Math 10 (App.): The advantage (scoring C+, B, or A) accorded to female students on the exam is *minus* 6 percent but in classrooms is plus 3 percent or *plus 9 percentage points*.
- Science 10: The advantage (scoring C+, B, or A) accorded to female students on the exam is 1 percent but in classrooms is 9 percent or *plus 8 percentage points*.
- Social Studies 11: The advantage (scoring C+, B, or A) accorded to female students on the exam is *minus* 1 percent but in classrooms is 13 percent or *plus 14 percentage points*.
- Civic Studies 11: The advantage (scoring C+, B, or A) accorded to female students on the exam is *minus* 1 percent but in classrooms is plus 18 percent or *plus 19 percentage points*.
- BC First Nations Studies: The advantage (scoring C+, B, or A) accorded to female students on the exam is 10 percent but in classrooms is 23 percent or *plus 13 percentage points*.
- English 12: The advantage (scoring C+, B, or A) accorded to female students on the exam is 8 percent and in classrooms is 12 percent or *plus 4 percentage points*.
- English 12, First Peoples: The advantage (scoring C+, B, or A) accorded to female students on the exam is 18 percent and in classrooms is 24 percent *or plus 6 percentage points*.
- Communications 12: The advantage (scoring C+, B, or A) accorded to female students on the exam is 3 percent and in classrooms is 14 percent *or plus 11 percentage points*.

In each subject, female students were given C+, B, or A marks more frequently than their male counterparts, which is not the issue. Rather, comparing these class marks with the provincial-examination marks reveals our concern that, when comparing the differences between class marks and provincial-examination marks, the female advantage was consistent. and the female advantage in provincial examinations was always by a considerably larger percentage. We can conclude that some teacher bias occurs, placing male students at a disadvantage whenever these assessments are used for awards, scholarships, and placement in university programs.

GENDER UNFAIRNESS IN ALBERTA

Alberta's student enrollment corresponds to that of a midsized state in the United States. Grade twelve students in Alberta write provincial school-leaving exit tests—the Diploma Examinations—after semesters in January and June. Marks on these examinations are combined with class marks from teachers for a final mark on the students' transcripts. An analysis for the standard of excellence and acceptable standard of 2016 marks based on gender follows *and records how many more female students than males achieved each standard. A negative sign depicts males having a higher percentage.* For example, in ELA 30-2, 67 percent more females received marks from their teacher denoting the student had achieved academic *excellence*. In the provincial exam, 26 percent more females received marks for excellence. The female advantage from their teachers' mark is 41 percent.

The *January results* (table 8.1) demonstrate how females were awarded more marks denoting they had achieved a standard of excellence from their teachers in *every subject*; however, females outscored the males only in five tests on the standardized provincial examinations marked *anonymously*. The prevalence of high marks from classroom teachers provided females an advantage in nine of the ten courses, and this advantage provides more opportunity for *awards, scholarships, and placement in university programs.* The overall advantage for females from high class marks is 15.9 percent.

The *June results* (table 8.2) demonstrate how females were awarded by their teachers more marks indicating they had achieved a *standard of excellence* in every subject; however, females outscored the males only in five tests on the standardized provincial examinations marked *anonymously*. The prevalence of high marks from classroom teachers provided females an advantage in nine of the ten courses, and this advantage provides more opportunity for awards, scholarships, and placement in university programs. The overall advantage for females from high class marks is 18.5 percent.

Combining the January and June test administrations reveals that female students were awarded more marks for achieving a standard of excellence in

Table 8.1. January 2016: Standard of Excellence (Equivalent to an A)

Subject	School Mark (%)	Diploma Examination Mark (%)	Female Advantage (%)
ELA 30-2	67	26	41
ELA 30-1	48	53	−5
Math 30-1	8	−5	13
Math 30-2	59	50	9
Biology	5	−4	9
Science	31	27	4
Chemistry	2	−7	9
Physics	13	1	12
Social Studies 30-1	19	−14	33
Social Studies 30-2	33	−1	34

nineteen of the twenty *classroom assessments*: June's chemistry marks proved the exception, with 0 percent advantage. However, using the system's Diploma Examinations, females and males had an equal number of test administrations with the higher percentage scoring a standard of excellence. Examining the upper-stream courses important for university applications, males outscored females at the standard of excellence on eight of the twelve administrations.

We next examined the data for students not achieving an acceptable standard. Table 8.3 shows our findings. For example, in ELA 30-2, 95 percent *more males* were assessed by their teachers as having failed. In the provincial exam, 13 percent more males failed. The female advantage from the school mark is 82 percent, where almost twice as few female students failed as did male students.

These January results demonstrate how females were *failed* less frequently by their teachers in every subject; however, females were failed at a higher percentage on three of the standardized provincial examinations marked anonymously. Viewing class marks and provincial tests together, the third column demonstrates how much females are advantaged by having such large discrepancies between the two types of assessments.

We then assessed the June results, as shown in table 8.4. For example, in ELA 30-2, 36 percent more males than females were assessed by their teacher as having failed. In the provincial exam, 12 percent more males failed. The female advantage from the school mark is 24 percent fewer failed.

These June results demonstrate how females were failed less frequently by their teachers in every subject; however, females were failed at a higher

Table 8.2. June 2016: Standard of Excellence (Equivalent to an A)

Subject	School Mark (%)	Diploma Examination Mark (%)	Female Advantage (%)
ELA 30-2	63	29	34
ELA 30-1	39	20	19
Math 30-1	6	−2	8
Math 30-2	40	56	−16
Biology	3	−7	10
Science	39	9	30
Chemistry	0	−15	15
Physics	15	0	15
Social Studies 30-1	15	−3	18
Social Studies 30-2	35	−1	36

percentage on five of the *standardized provincial examinations marked anonymously*. Viewing class marks and provincial tests together, the third column demonstrates how much females are advantaged by having such large discrepancies between the two types of assessments. High levels of grade inflation evident within class assessments by teachers, *who are not marking students anonymously*, compensate females' lower achievement on provincial standardized tests.

Notably, on Social Studies 30-1, females were failed in their class marks less frequently than males by 30 percent; however, on the provincial Diploma Examination, females failed 31 percent more frequently, which placed them at an overall disadvantage by 1 percent. In physics classes, females' classroom failure rates were 124 percent lower than the rate for males; yet female students failed the Diploma Examination more frequently (6 percent) but still were advantaged by 118 percent fewer failures when combining the two sets of marks.

It is also noteworthy that on the twenty examinations during these two semesters, only on two occasions—that is, in ELA 30-1, at −5 percent, and in Math 30-2, at −16 percent—were females disadvantaged when comparing marks awarded on the provincial examinations denoting that the student had achieved a standard of excellence. Females were disadvantaged only in one subject (Social Studies 30-1, at −1 percent) when conducting a similar comparison combining marks for meeting the acceptable standard.

In the run-up to the provincial election in 2015, the government sought to pander to the teachers' union support by altering the weighting of the two components leading to students' final marks. The standard through many

Table 8.3. January 2016: Not achieving the acceptable standard (did not meet and therefore must retake the course)

Subject	School Mark (%)	Diploma Examination Mark (%)	Female Advantage (%)
ELA 30-2	−95	−13	82
ELA 30-1	−110	−8	102
Math 30-1	−42	−1	41
Math 30-2	−67	−36	31
Biology	−9	4	13
Science	−92	−2	90
Chemistry	−12	−2	10
Physics	−128	−13	115
Social Studies 30-1	−17	27	44
Social Studies 30-2	−42	17	59

decades was to weight the class marks equally (50/50) with the provincial Diploma Examination. Beginning in 2016, the government *implemented a new weighting, with class marks accounting for 70 percent, making this component more than twice the value of the provincial tests*, which were professionally prepared, extensively field tested, and marked anonymously.

Table 8.5 provides an example of how the new formula (70/30) further exaggerates the advantage females enjoyed in the marks for standards of excellence achieved in January 2016 exams (which was displayed earlier in table 8.1).

The revised blended grading instituted by government is misleading, particularly when the school-awarded mark and Diploma Examination marks diverge. An e-mail received from the provincial examination manager revealed one troubling situation within a school:

> [There was one] class averaging over 80% on the school-awarded mark and less than 50% on the Diploma Examination mark. The resulting blended average; a grade likely in the low 70% range (under the new 70/30 blend) *is not the result of any assessment evidence justifying this grade*, yet this grade could be used to determine a student's post-secondary eligibility.

Grade inflation occurring in classrooms further inflated by a factor of 2.3 in the 70/30 newly adopted *weighting regime clearly identifies which gender will win future awards, scholarships, and placements in university programs.*

For example, Alberta has two major universities—in Edmonton and Calgary—and their undergraduate enrollment already reports a decided advan-

Table 8.4. June 2016: Not achieving the acceptable standard (did not meet and therefore must retake the course)

Subject	School Mark (%)	Diploma Examination Mark (%)	Female Advantage (%)
ELA 30-2	−36	−12	24
ELA 30-1	−43	−4	39
Math 30-1	−48	2	50
Math 30-2	−55	−30	25
Biology	−6	3	9
Science	−62	−1	61
Chemistry	−20	12	32
Physics	−124	−6	118
Social Studies 30-1	−30	31	−1
Social Studies 30-2	−57	11	68

tage for female students. According to recent data reported by the University of Alberta in Edmonton, for example, 12,962 males and 16,138 females were registered for the fall 2010 term (University of Alberta, 2011), meaning females accounted for 55.5 percent of placements. The University of Calgary's 2015 report put placements at 10,667 males and 12,146 females, meaning 53.3 percent of all placements were awarded to female students. *The female ratio will increase substantially with the government's decision to weight class marks higher by a factor of 2.3:1.*

GRADE INFLATION'S GENDER ADVANTAGE

The foregoing provides evidence of the female gender advantage in British Columbia and Alberta, two high-achieving school systems on the *PISA 2015 assessments of fifteen-year-old* students. The problem of grade inflation demands we ask whether every student has an inflated mark or only some students. Unfairness occurs when different criteria are used when students' work is assessed.

The Fraser Institute in Canada routinely posts reviews on their website for provincial test results demonstrating gender differences in *elementary school* grades in three provinces: British Columbia, Alberta, and Ontario. The institute also posted a review of Quebec's *secondary school* results. These reviews for the 2014–2015 school year compare percentages of schools across the respective provinces where one gender's achievement in language arts (reading) and mathematics was highest:

Table 8.5. January 2016: Standard of excellence (equivalent to an A) with impact of 70/30 weighting in favor of class mark indicated in brackets and bold print

Subject	School Mark (%)	Diploma Examination Mark (%)	Female Advantage (%)
ELA 30-2	67 (154)	26	41 (128)
ELA 30-1	48 (110)	53	−5 (57)
Math 30-1	8 (23)	−5	13 (23)
Math 30-2	59 (136)	50	9 (86)
Biology	5 (12)	−4	9 (16)
Science	31 (71)	27	4 (44)
Chemistry	2 (5)	−7	9 (12)
Physics	13 (30)	1	12 (31)
Social Studies 30-1	19 (44)	−14	33 (58)
Social Studies 30-2	33 (76)	−1	34 (75)

- Ontario (Grade 6): The reading gender gap favored females at 71.7 percent of schools, males at 13.8 percent of schools, and was even at 14.5 percent of schools. The math gender gap favored females at 45.6 percent of schools, males at 40.5 percent of schools, and was even at 13.9 percent schools.
- British Columbia (Grade 7): The reading gender gap favored females at 62.7 percent of schools, males at 36.7 percent of schools, and was even at 0.6 percent of schools. The math gender gap favored females at 36.7 percent of schools, males at 62.1 percent of schools, and was even at 1.2 percent schools.
- Alberta (Grade 6): The language arts gender gap favored females at 88.8 percent of schools, males at 10.9 percent of schools, and was even at 0.3 percent of schools. The math gender gap favored males at 49.4 percent of schools, females at 49.7 percent of schools, and was even at 0.9 percent of schools.
- Quebec (Secondary): In language of instruction, females scored the highest in 95 percent of schools, while males scored highest in 72 percent of schools in mathematics. (Adapted from Cowley and Easton, 2014)

These comparisons, reflecting percentages of schools rather than percentages of students, *overwhelmingly favor female results on reading standardized tests*. Dueck (2018) provides a partial explanation for these results based on research indicating the advantage female students enjoy from learning in classrooms dominated by female teachers. The head start female students gain from these early years can remain through to the end of school; however, the paucity of male teachers in the primary grades makes it virtually impossible to assess the impact they have on male students.

In mathematics, the percentages of schools where male students scored higher levels of achievement on system tests were substantially different in British Columbia and Quebec. In tables 8.1 and 8.2, which compared marks for Mathematics 30-1 (the upper-stream course), males scored marginally higher than females on the Diploma Examination, while females received higher results from their classroom teachers. The advantage for females was 13 percent in the January testing and 8 percent in June testing. A record of classroom marks for a comparison with test results is not provided by the Fraser Institute.

In addition to the analysis of gender-based learning undertaken by the Fraser Institute, Voyer (2014) writes of a *meta-analysis* taken from 308 studies reflecting grades of 538,710 boys and 595,332 girls. Seventy percent of the samples consisted of students from the United States, with the remainder coming from more than thirty other countries. Voyer assessed the meta-analysis's conclusions, which found that

> Although gender differences follow essentially stereotypical patterns on achievement tests in which boys typically score higher on math and science, females have the advantage on school grades regardless of the material. School marks reflect learning in the larger social context of the classroom and require effort and persistence over long periods of time, whereas standardized tests assess basic or specialized academic abilities and aptitudes at one point in time without social influences.
>
> Based on research from 1914 through 2011 that spanned more than 30 countries, the study found the differences in grades between girls and boys were largest for language courses and smallest for math and science. The female advantage in school performance in math and science did not become apparent until junior or middle school. The degree of gender difference in grades increased from elementary to middle school but decreased between high school and college.
>
> The study reveals that recent claims of a "boy crisis," with boys lagging behind girls in school achievement, are not accurate, because girls' grades have been consistently higher than boys' across several decades with no significant changes in recent years, the authors wrote.
>
> The fact that females generally perform better than their male counterparts throughout what is essentially mandatory schooling in most countries seems to be a well-kept secret, considering how little attention it has received as a global phenomenon.
>
> As for why girls perform better in school than boys, the authors speculated that social and cultural factors could be among several possible explanations. Parents may assume boys are better at math and science, so they might encourage girls to put more effort into their studies, which could lead to the slight advantage girls have in all courses. Gender differences in learning styles is another possibility. Previous research has shown girls tend to study in order to

understand the materials, whereas boys emphasize performance, which indicates a focus on the final grades. Mastery of the subject matter generally produces better marks than performance emphasis, so this could account in part for males' lower marks than females.

Voyer's analysis is important, because the meta-analysis findings are based on data from many different scholastic cultures worldwide in addition to the predominantly American students. The conclusion is that females perennially—actually, for many decades—have received *higher marks from classroom teachers* and that these differences are greatest in language arts and that, therefore, a "boy crisis" based on student academic achievement is not an issue because the phenomenon is not recent.

A similar conclusion is evident in Voyer's statement speculating that "social and cultural factors could be among several possible explanations." Here we come to the specific purpose for this chapter: Incorporating social and cultural factors in students' classroom grading opens the door to *subjectivity* when assessing academic achievement. In other words, teacher bias is introduced when these factors become part of the assessment process, and a message in this chapter is that *assessments of learning should not be conflated with behavior or cultural issues.*

Douglas Reeves, an American expert on academic assessment, provided an insightful exchange of e-mails to me, telling me that, "The teacher bias that I have observed is most insidious not in the tests themselves but in the conflation of academic performance and behavior when translating test performance into marks for the report card." If behavior influences student letter grades, are there some whose behavior advantages them more than others?

If there is a discernible pattern demonstrating a bias, then the issue of fairness rears its ugly head. Reeves explains that

> Students (disproportionately minority girls, in my research) receive higher letter grades for lower actual achievement because of their quiet, compliant, and respectful attitude. I will note, parenthetically, that I'm all in favor of quiet, compliant, and respectful behavior among teenagers; I just wish that we would not call these characteristics "algebra" or "physics."

Webber et al. (2009) similarly concluded that culture influenced student marks. "Almost 60 percent of educators," the write, "perceived that students' cultural background affected the grades these students got."

Reeves explains further in his e-mails to me how the bias serves to *disadvantage male students*, adding the observation that teachers readily discern a dichotomy between test and class marks:

> Other students (disproportionately boys) receive lower letter grades for higher actual achievement because of disorganization and oppositional behavior.

Every time I ask teachers if they can think of students who make A's and B's on tests yet receive D's or F's in the class, almost every hand goes up.

Harlen (2004), synthesizing *twenty-three studies* from the United Kingdom and the United States, also concluded that evidence of gender bias exists, finding that "Teachers' judgments of the academic performance of young children are influenced by the teachers' assessment of their behavior; this adversely affects the assessment of boys compared with girls." Scantlebury (2009) stated it somewhat differently: "Overall," she writes, "teachers have lower expectations for girls' academic success compared to boys" (n.p.).

Webber et al. (2009), after surveying and interviewing teachers, found that a surprisingly high percentage of teachers acknowledged a *gender bias*:

Almost 1 in 4 (23%) of educators agree "students' gender" affects the grades they get. However, qualitative data suggests that frequently gender was linked with behavior, in that boys were perceived to be more likely to be disruptive and less compliant, which in turn influenced the grades that teachers assigned to boys.

In other words, while only one in four teachers *openly* acknowledged gender bias, the interview process revealed the potential for boys to be disadvantaged when having their work assessed because of their *lower levels of compliant behavior*.

It is discouraging to think that biases based on gender could find a way into our school system. We expect fairness and consistency to be foundational in our society, and yet *we don't expect it to occur in our classrooms*. Some stakeholders may feel defensive about this unacceptable situation, and so the *regional* study delved into this issue at considerable length by assessing gender bias for students from *grade 1 through to university*.

In our region's mathematics tests, male students scored higher on grades 3, 6, and 9 system tests at both the acceptable standard and standard of excellence. When teachers were required to report on student report cards, their *classroom assessments* of student achievement in grades 1 through 9, more males were assessed as functioning *below grade level in every grade*. In these evaluations, students' final marks were based exclusively on the teachers' assessment without knowing how students performed on the standardized tests, because these system tests were given in the final week of the school year after report cards were already completed.

At the end of grade 9, students *self-selected* a mathematics stream for senior high school that would lead to university programing. Unfortunately for male students, programing decisions are made in April for the following September, but, since system tests occur at the end of June, *classroom marks weigh heavily in decisions*. Students and their parents did not receive their grade 9 system test results until the end of September, well after they had begun their grade 10 course. Participation rates in the grade 10 *upper-stream mathematics course* favored females even though males demonstrated higher proficiency on the system tests.

This aspect of the study is significant because grade 10 programing is the first screen in choosing a career. Enrolling in the lower-stream mathematics course curtails qualification for university acceptance and, coincidentally, career aspirations. Mathematics is a significant *gatekeeper into the world of work*, and the screening process, influenced by the biases presented, is eliminating many males from contention.

Experiencing a disadvantage in *gaining placement* in upper-stream mathematics courses, male students continue to experience a negative bias, further limiting their potential for scholarships and acceptance by universities. In this study, school-awarded marks and examination marks each count for 50 percent of the final course mark, and more female students received the standard of excellence from the school-awarded marks, while more males received this high standard on the Diploma Examination. *This pattern of assessment was consistent over a period of seven consecutive semesters.*

From a broader perspective of examining all courses in English, mathematics, sciences, and social studies, the analysis underscores an advantage for female students. *Aggregating seven consecutive semesters* across these courses—seventy tests—females received *almost double* the A marks received by males from teachers' *class marks*—that is, females received 13.3 percent of A's, while 6.7 percent of males received A's. Diploma Examination marks told a different story, as male students scoring A marks averaged 8.7 percent, while females were at 9.0 percent. When combining, and weighing, both sets of marks equally, females held a substantial advantage gleaned from their high set of classroom marks.

Considering only the *upper-stream courses*, which are critical determinants for accessing universities, school-level A marks were 66 percent more frequent than were Diploma Examination A marks, which demonstrates the high level of grade inflation for these important subjects. *Classroom*-level A marks favored females by 11.4 percent, while *examination* A marks favored males by 8.1 percent. Since the data set demonstrates significant grade inflation at the school level, females receive substantial advantage in securing scholarships and placements into prestigious universities.

A superintendent, who became aware of these disturbing trends, undertook a study in his school district. He tracked all student marks by gender as they progressed through high school and monitored trends as students went from classrooms taught by teachers of one gender to classrooms taught by teachers of the other. His review revealed a disturbing fact: Female students going from a grade where the teacher was a female to a grade where the teacher was a male experienced a *bump-up* in their marks. While males progressing from a male to a female teacher also benefitted, the bump-up was not significant. When the superintendent apprised his principals with these findings, he was greatly disturbed by their responses. They readily acknowledged the situation and referred to it as the "halter-top effect." This sad revelation underscores how bias can intervene in efforts to ensure fairness for students.

The advantage for female students evident in the regional study also translated into the 2007 Statistics Canada national report for Canada, *Why Are Most University Students Women*. "The gap in university attendance," this study found,

> is largely associated with differences in academic performance and study habits at the age of 15, parental expectations, and other characteristics of men and women. . . . Weaker academic performance among men accounted for almost one-half (45%) of the gap. Specifically, young men had lower overall school marks at age 15 and had poorer performance on a standardized reading test. . . .
>
> In the 2001 Census, universities had clearly become the domain of women, as they made up 58 percent of all graduates. . . .
>
> We find the that differences in the characteristics of boys and girls account for more than three quarters (76.8%) of the gap in university participation. In order of importance, the main factors are differences in school marks at age 15 (31.8%), standardized test scores in reading at age 15 (14.6%), study habits (11.1 %), parental expectations (8.5 %), and the university earnings premium relative to high school (5.3 %). (Frenette & Zeman, 2007, p. 5)

The *school mark* is the leading contributor for answering why most university students in Canada are women. The message in this study is made more significant when we factor in that most Canadian students progressing from high school to university submit marks only generated by their teachers. In other words, most provinces do not have exit examinations in grade 12, which could counterbalance the biased marks from teachers. The "weaker academic performance among men" is a significant factor, given the evidence that demonstrates *their marks are impacted negatively by noncompliant behaviors.*

When the school system does not implement *standardized testing accompanied by anonymous marking*, male students are disadvantaged when seeking entry into universities. York University in Ontario already is reporting their enrollment at 70 percent female, which is significant, because Ontario suffers from the highest levels of grade inflation in Canada. *The higher the rate of grade inflation, the greater the potential for female acceptance into universities because of their more-compliant school behaviors.*

This disadvantage is corroborated in the United States by another study released in an October 2006 article in the *American School Board Journal*, where the authors suggested what administrators might find when examining their districts:

> Boys, they'll probably notice, make up 80 to 90 percent of the district's discipline referrals, 70 percent of learning-disabled children, and at least two-thirds of the children on behavioral medication. They'll probably find that boys earn two-thirds of the Ds and Fs in the district, but less than half the As. (Gurian & Stevens, 2007)

In our regional study, three times as many male students were coded with moderate or severe disabilities, and two times more with mild or moderate disabilities. At the same time, males coded with different types of disabilities generally *tended to outperform* coded females when teachers assessed their grade level of achievement. *In other words, more male students were identified as having special needs but assessed as demonstrating higher achievement by teachers.* An obvious question is whether all of these males should have been coded or they were behaving differently than the girls in a female-dominated world. Definitely, *caring about fairness for boys and girls specifically is a transformational issue for education.*

A message in the previous chapter is that grade inflation resulting from low standards or low expectations teachers have of their students is a significant problem. Students and their parents receive false information about how well their child is learning the academic curriculum. This misleading information instills a *false sense of security* in students, who then lose some of their motivation to contribute their best effort to their studies. Ultimately, taxpayers are robbed of having students prepared to a level that will maximize potential.

A second message follows the first but that should increase the trepidation we have toward the effectiveness of our school system. *Grade inflation is not equally applied across all students but, rather, favors the female gender with an advantage in securing awards, scholarships, and placement in prestigious university programs.* This disadvantage to male students may be unfair, but it is disregarded and kept hidden from public scrutiny because educators do not want to lose the confidence of taxpayers and their government representatives.

For teachers and their unions, the alternative to resolving this unfairness is unpalatable acquiescence to use of standardized testing where individual control over construction of the assessment is lost and students' anonymity is ensured. Perhaps of even greater importance is that any use of standardized testing permits higher levels of accountability for results, and such increased transparency for system quality not only has implications for the educators but also for the politicians responsible for the school system.

Provincial officers must ensure that politicians are knowledgeable about this significant concern, which requires the courage and diligence to speak truth to power. It is more pleasurable to engage in complimentary dialogue than expose concerns demonstrating unfairness to students. Ensuring that our political leaders hear and understand the implications of the truth is a responsibility required of education's leadership in school districts and regional governments.

The key points made in this chapter follow:

- British Columbia and Alberta, high performing provinces on PISA assessments, are plagued with high levels of grade inflation in classroom marks compared with marks for Diploma Examinations, which favor female students.
- Several Canadian provinces demonstrate grade inflation at the classroom level, favoring female students in middle school grades.
- Conclusions in a meta-analysis of research concludes that females perennially receive—and for many decades since have received—*higher marks from classroom teachers* and that these differences are greatest in language arts classes.
- The meta-analysis concludes that *social and cultural factors* have a role in female students receiving higher classroom marks, which is an unacceptable state of affairs.
- Bias against male students is a worldwide phenomenon.
- This disadvantage toward male students may be unfair, but it is disregarded and kept hidden from public scrutiny because educators do not want to lose the confidence of taxpayers and their government representatives.

Chapter Nine

Superintendent Leadership

Adopting a teacher of teachers' perspective is a fundamental responsibility for school principals, and working as a principal of principals is a critical function assigned to the district superintendent. As stressed earlier, as the principal goes, so goes the school. And this chapter progresses to the next level, illustrating that as the superintendent goes, so goes the school district. Leadership is not merely in a person's title but, rather, how that person acts in accordance with their title.

INSTRUCTIONAL LEADERSHIP

Earlier, we spoke of the principal willing to take the risk by videotaping their own classroom work for analysis by other teachers. Venturing to become the movie's main character is an example of how leadership can be jeopardized by an ill-fated gamble. Leadership, like beauty, is in the eye of the beholder when analyzing someone's professional performance.

Just as teachers appreciate seeing their principal in action, so can superintendents enhance their image as instructional leaders by assuming an expectation assigned to principals. Providing feedback to teachers is a critical responsibility for principals and, therefore, a function each superintendent can model. Watching a tape of a conference following a classroom observation earned respect from principals because they readily understood the risk associated with this venture. It also paved the way for principals to volunteer having their debriefing sessions taped for viewing by colleagues as the next phase of instructional leadership.

Chapter 9

VISIBLE LEADERSHIP

Visibility in classrooms is a major responsibility for school principals, and this same concept is applicable at the district level for the superintendent and schools within the district. The goal I have set for myself was to visit more than 1,000 classrooms and 400 schools annually, and I managed to exceed these goals every year. Eventually, more than 20,000 classrooms were visited, providing immense understanding of how education was delivered. Maintaining a record of these visits is as necessary a function as the principal's maintaining a personal record of informal visits to classrooms.

Supervisory visits to a school were both scheduled and unscheduled. If the latter, the visit was only with the school administration or for a school-wide event—for example, on sports day, for Christmas concerts, and so on. The informal meetings with school administration enhanced communication between the district office and school administration by providing an opportunity to discuss issues the principal was facing but otherwise would not have bothered to contact district administration to discuss. Spending time in the evenings when school-wide concerts or other programs were held for parents enhanced the district/school relationship because teachers witnessed their superintendent spending personal time celebrating their efforts.

These impromptu visits were low anxiety; however, supervisory visits to classrooms are not. These are important for superintendent's understanding of the current educational environment as well as monitoring the teaching strategies employed. Therefore, notifying school principals of a superintendent tour of classrooms two days in advance is advisable. The situation is real and authentic because notification merely identifies the day and not the schedule.

The benefit these visits have to district morale is astounding when accompanied with feedback. The extensive feedback focused on elements for effective teaching the superintendent was able to observe during the classroom visit. In other words, the superintendent was able to go into great detail when affirming the teacher's pedagogy. Developing this compendium required many hours of detailed and thoughtful consideration on the part of the superintendent.

When the brief classroom observation was concluded, the primary task for the superintendent was to identify, at minimum, one element of teaching efficacy for comment. After the visitations were concluded, the superintendent followed up in two ways: First, the principal was told which teaching element had been identified for each teacher and was asked whether this finding was consistent with the principal's own observations. Mixed messaging cannot occur, especially if the principal is conducting a performance evaluation with a staff member. The second follow-up was to provide some form of positive feedback to the observed teacher; just as positive feedback should follow impromptu observation, so should support be offered after a scheduled observation. A secretary, with access to the compendium of comments pertaining to the elements of effective teaching, received the list of teachers visited that day and the element being recognized. Within a few minutes, the secretary was able to craft an individualized note and prepare it for signature and delivery; a copy was always sent to the principal. Extensive preparation ensured that the notes, far from feeling like form letters, were unique and meaningful for each staff member who received one.

A further benefit to the superintendent quickly became evident from this approach. Logically, evidence of district-wide professional development—that is, personalized learning, cooperative learning, questioning techniques, and so on—should be evident in some classrooms. An informal assessment from district in-service or professional development is readily discerned when the superintendent spends time in classrooms.

SCHOOL GOAL SETTING

Just as personal goal setting is an annual activity requiring a beginning and concluding session, school goal setting requires the same diligence. Workload issues must be considered because the school district may have too many schools for the superintendent's direct involvement. The value of these sessions means I made a personal commitment to meet with all fifty schools and to include the appropriate assistant superintendent as well as other district officers with specific interests in specific schools.

A number of school-level goals are worth consideration:

- Professional-development needs for all or specific groups of staff
- Community and parent involvement
- Student leadership and participation
- Student achievement, including scholarship
- Student attitudes, behavior, and attendance
- Program implementation
- And professional buddy initiatives within the school or with other schools.

Goal setting and assessing outcomes must be professional twins. The exercise is meaningful when measures for each goal are determined during the goal-setting process. While the list of measures can be modified during the year, the initial event of outlining goals must be accompanied with measures and appropriate targets.

It is vital to the success of the entire goal setting process and celebration that realistic targets for each measure are identified. It's a natural tendency for some people to overestimate how much improvement is realistic when setting goals for themselves. For example, when pressing them as to whether or not it's realistic for them to move from 65 percent efficacy to 100 percent efficacy in a skill in the space of one academic year, they may say, "Of course we want everyone to achieve the outcome." But more careful consideration might reveal that such lofty target could perhaps be realistically attained over five years of hard work, and poorly setting unattainable goals only leads to frustration.

An even greater concern is when, during the year-end review, outcomes have not even been measured: the evaluation process has been sidestepped even though the measurement process was carefully reviewed during the initial meeting when the goals were first established. Leadership has to be questioned in such cases when the critical conclusion is avoided.

This unfortunate situation with avoiding measurement became an issue in the early years in my career as superintendent when goal setting was first introduced in my schools. It was obvious in meeting with fifty schools that some staff members were more committed to the process than others. The education system was expending public funds, and taxpayers deserved knowing that their contribution was making a difference. For centuries this information was anecdotal, with vague interpretation; what was described as excellent in one environment was only passable in another because standards were not enunciated.

Therefore, commitment to achieving goals was haphazard. In some instances, these documented goals were referenced routinely, while in others the carefully crafted documents gathered dust on top of a cupboard. In an effort to reward stewardship of public funds, we established an incentive program for achieving targets. Thirteen of fifty schools chose to participate, while the other thirty-seven opted out, mostly because of union opposition. Targets for each goal were negotiated with the superintendent, and, amazingly, the only modifications to targets were downward, reflecting a concern that staff had perhaps been hoping for too much improvement too quickly.

In the final analysis at the year's end, each of the thirteen schools achieved all of their targets and conducted public ceremonies with their community when they were awarded additional funding to pursue the following year's targets. These celebrations included parents, and the excitement associated with success was gratifying. Measuring was a new concept in education and an associated risk was a concern.

However, while a $5,000 recognition for good stewardship made the exercise worthwhile for thirteen of the schools, we were disappointed with the result in the other thirty-seven schools. In these not one goal was achieved or celebrated, because none of the goals had actually been measured. Recall that this was in the early days of goal setting, and, in fact, much work was necessary to combat indifference to the new initiative. Naturally, the school's follow-through and successes in the goal-setting activity were reflected in the principal's performance evaluation.

CLUSTER SCHOOLS

Every student should benefit from participating in a comprehensive school program with highly qualified teachers. Opportunity to have such expertise available in smaller schools is less likely, because specialist teachers look for full-time assignments in their specialized area of expertise, but providing students with expert teachers for all subjects simply cannot be accommodated in smaller schools unless the specialist has multidisciplinary expertise. District superintendents have an obligation to incorporate organizational designs that ensure all students have a fair opportunity to experience programs enhancing their various levels of intelligence.

Students' talent in musicality, visualization, linguistics, reasoning, athletics, socialization, and introspection are considered by developmental psychologist Howard Gardner (1983) to represent seven of the intelligence modalities, each of which should be addressed to hook students into their ongoing education. Too many students miss out when opportunity with a specialist is not available because the school has too few teachers equipped with some measure of these specialties.

This lack of fairness to students can be resolved when administrators attach schools together with staff assignments in more than one school. In our case, five small schools within several miles of each other were hooked into a cluster arrangement under one supervising principal and a vice principal responsible for each facility. Similar arrangements are possible with a large school clustered with one or two small neighboring schools.

Each school in our cluster worked with specialist teachers in music, art, mathematics, language arts, French, science, and physical education. Each program provided students with an enrichment experience and periodically brought everyone together for concerts, art and science shows, and various sporting events. Parents were thrilled with this arrangement because they recognized how their child experienced an enriched educational program beyond what would have been available in even a large school.

Providing such an opportunity required one simple strategy: Teachers rather than students traveled between schools. Aligning school schedules allowed recess- and noon-hour travel by specialists, whom we reimbursed for the travel and who were excited by the opportunity to have a teaching load exclusively aligned with their interests and talents. Preparations and planning were minimized because their materials and activities were useable at each school. Staff turnover was almost nonexistent because none of the specialists left once this arrangement was made.

DISTRICT PARENT ADVISORY COUNCIL (DPAC)

Parent advisory councils—or PACs—are a relatively common organizational bodies comprised across school systems, and superintendents will benefit by incorporating a district parent advisory council—or DPAC. Each PAC is represented at the DPAC, which is focused on providing the superintendent with advice and is authorized to vote on issues related to the district's operation. The superintendent can relate the DPAC's advice to the school board during its policy deliberations, and these parent representatives complete the communication cycle by informing local PACs of the school board's decisions.

Communications from DPAC to PAC might include:

- Information about the district budget and district-wide initiatives
- Policy and regulations approved by the school board
- Curriculum changes and implications
- District performance of the district report card or measurement program
- The district's perspective on unanticipated issues reported in the media
- Unraveling political jargon about education
- Reporting analyses of district studies—that is, grade inflation, suspensions, attendance, etc.
- And how to prepare for productive parent/teacher conferences.

COMMUNITY PRESENTATIONS

In addition to the interaction with DPACs, the superintendent provides a critical role in garnering public support for the community's school system. Many community clubs—Rotary, Lions, and so on—provide a podium for their community's chief educator when information about the school district's performance and goals can be presented. These sessions also provide opportunities to hear and respond to people's issues even though they may no longer have children in the school system.

Newspapers provide another method for presenting to the general public regarding the school system's performance and issues. While serving as district superintendent, a weekly column in the local newspaper reported on similar issues presented to the DPAC, as well as demystifying educational issues floating about in the general public. At any given time, a number of important issues were relevant, meaning these editorials were informative and, when necessary, provocative.

One district newspaper conducted research on the community's leaders by displaying their headshots, focusing only on each individual's nose and mouth. Despite having served in the community for less than three years and having the shortest tenure of all others, the poll determined the superintendent's image as the second-most recognizable, ahead of all the political leadership except the long-serving mayor.

SCHOOL-BASED DECISION MAKING (SBDM)

When I was serving as principal, my school proposed to the superintendent that we determine for ourselves whether a teacher's absence actually warranted the use of a substitute teacher and, if not, that we could delay using that substitute-teacher service for a later date—in other words, banking substitute-teacher services for later use. Such a request had never been made before, and so the district okayed our request as a pilot program to determine value for dollar. It turned out that on many occasions, especially when our teachers took half-days for medical appointments, and even on some occasions when ancillary teachers were absent, we were able to make internal arrangements within the school that negated the requirement for a substitute teacher.

These banked days provided teams of teachers the opportunity to employ substitute teachers for special classroom projects. On certain theme days they created for their students, for example, teachers were able to break the class up into smaller groups and call on additional teacher aides to facilitate some of these smaller groups. Further, when all-day field trips were scheduled, additional teachers could be hired for the day to reduce the supervisory workload.

A few years later, after I had become superintendent, our district implemented full SBDM; we were only the third school district in Canada to empower schools with such authority. Schools received an allocation and could spend their funding on human resources and materials. We made two major discoveries immediately—and over time these observed changes proved lasting.

The first thing we noticed with the implementation of full SBDM was that budget surpluses at year-end in individual school accounts replaced the zero-dollar accounts we'd seen previously. In other words, the wild spending in the final month of a budget year no longer occurred because SBDM allowed schools to carry forward their surplus from year to year. Storerooms overfilled with supplies that might not have been used for several years were replaced with supplies sufficient to meet short-term needs. Planned expenditures replaced frantic buying.

The second outcome was the most dramatic. With the implementation of full SBDM, teacher absenteeism dropped significantly, because staff realized a benefit directly if they scheduled appointments for times when school was not in session. Yes, it was the case that some staff who otherwise believed that sick relief was an entitlement to be used monthly regardless of whether they were truly ill did feel peer pressure to be at work. But we soon found that our rates of absenteeism reflected greater consistency with the staff absenteeism seen in private-sector organizations. Later, a new administration was able to withdraw substitute services from school budgets entirely, producing a substantial cost increase of almost 40 percent for the district.

Holding schools accountable for their results is a key point in this discussion. Holding school staff accountable for outcomes is considerably more difficult when not accompanied with SBDM. A cookie-cutter approach to resourcing schools reduces ingenuity in schools experiencing significant obstacles for improving student success.

CHAIN OF COMMAND

The superintendent's visibility in the community is a valuable asset to the school system, but it actually can create a potential disruption to the established chain of command. Parents, upset by an issue at their school, are emboldened to bypass the school and contact a superintendent who has made themselves more available and visible. Community and parental concerns cannot be brushed aside, because the superintendent's credibility is at stake, which can be communicated quickly through the school district's unofficial pipeline.

Providing assurance to principals that the chain of command will be followed is the first step toward resolving this concern. Conflict resolution requires that complainants never meet a dead end but always have another court of appeal available. Therefore, the superintendent's discussion with principals should include expectations for providing parents with the name and contact information for the next person in line for an appeal.

Such openness with parents frequently resolves the issue, because principals endeavor to accomplish resolution without moving it up the chain. When another channel for communicating their grievance is provided, the complainant understands that the principal is giving attention to their concern because reversing a decision can be embarrassing.

Reminding a concerned parent to first seek a resolution with the principal gently clarifies everyone of the chain of command, even as it reassures the complainant that the appropriate supervisors are aware of the specific issue. And reinforcing the chain of command—reiterating district policy that concerns be addressed with the school before involving the district office—establishes the principle that the best resolutions occur with staff nearest to the problem. Leap-frogging the chain of command produces tension and backlash within the district in addition to a distrustful relationship between home and school. If the complainant cannot articulate evidence that the chain of command was followed, they are reminded to return to the appropriate person.

When the complainant has followed due process and is appealing to the superintendent, preparing for the ensuing conference requires that the superintendent have appropriate background information from the previous administrator in the chain. After presenting their perspective, the complainant should summarize their understanding why those in the chain of command are holding fast to the decision. This meeting does not conclude until the complainant willingly drops their concern because they now have a better understanding of the decision made.

Otherwise, if the complainant does not drop the concern, the superintendent assures the complainant of follow-up discussion with the previous reviewer and an approximate time when the next meeting will be held for discussing a final administrative decision. This assurance also informs the complainant that an appeal can be presented to the school board for final resolution.

When my district adhered to this policy for dealing with complaints, we saw a dramatic reduction in grievances coming to the superintendent's office. Equally important was that in a certain three-year period we had only one complaint go to the school board, and this particular issue concerned the school district's lack of busing to a remote corner of the district.

PRINCIPAL PROFESSIONAL DEVELOPMENT

Just as the school administrator has the responsibility to engineer professional development for teachers, the superintendent is responsible to ensure that school principals receive ongoing in-services. One strategy employs district officials meeting with principals for the purpose of updating their information needs related to curriculum changes, new policies, and public relations, among other issues.

A more profound development program ensures that *teachers teach students, principals teach teachers, and superintendents teach principals.* In other words, we recognize that as the superintendent goes, so goes the school district. This section provides four examples for how superintendents can facilitate leadership development for principals and other district administrators.

The first way a superintendent develops principals engages many of the district's principals—if not all of them, depending on the district's size—in a project focusing on what a principal's role really is. This committee of principals itemizes the various responsibilities of a principal that have been identified in research as well as through local surveys. Threats and opportunities associated with each identified responsibility are reviewed for presentation and discussion with the entire group of administrators. Recommendations that emerge from the group are then presented to the superintendent and school board. The district's chief administrator does not personally engage in this activity but envisions its potential use for further action within the district.

The second effective strategy for developing a district's principals employs a regular scheduling of group activities. At least once per month, administrators meet to learn about new leadership ideas circulating through the literature. These ideas may relate to new studies regarding learning styles or leadership styles and behaviors. The onus for these sessions rests on the superintendent who leads activities emanating from personal and current learning. In other words, the superintendent accepts responsibility for identifying emerging learning in order to contribute to the development of others.

These sessions also are useful for examining schools' assessments of student learning, as outlined in a previous chapter. District results are the superintendent's focus in these sessions when trends are viewed related to grade inflation, gender differences, student retention, and acceleration, along with other relevant trends. Modeling the analysis at the district level then guides principals in reviewing local results with their school staff.

A third opportunity for principal development is found in personal meetings hosted by the superintendent. Whether these are breakfast or lunch meetings or are held at other times during the workday, superintendents can use these get-togethers to discuss the principal's skills, knowledge, and understandings of their many roles. Further, this one-to-one event provides opportunity to discuss aspirations for advancement as well as problems experienced within the school. These sessions can also provide discussion of a particular leadership book distributed for this purpose to all administrators. Professional bonding between superintendent and individual administrators is the critical benefit in this approach.

A fourth component of a superintendent's development of the district's principals paralleled the Gallup Organization's (2002) use by principals of the previously mentioned Teacher Perceiver Instrument (see chapter 5 for an in-depth discussion). At the superintendent level, however, the focus is on developing principal talent, which the Principal Perceiver addresses. Over a period of years, the superintendent interacts with this tool to focus on the individual's leadership strengths and weaknesses using a well-researched approach.

This chapter identifies strategies superintendents can employ as the community's educational leader. Visibility in schools and in the public eye are important to building confidence sufficient to enhance accountability and transparency as well as quell turbulent times and parent complaints.

The next chapter presents a controversial issue that suggests why principals should be removed from a commonly held but poorly administered role.

If a desired goal is to ensure students receive the best education, then it is incumbent upon leadership to ensure that students are educated by the best teachers.

Chapter Ten

Coaches Are Not Reliable Evaluators

We cannot trust the judgment of even well-intentioned people if they are not good at what they are doing. Effective, highly interactive cultures incorporate pressure and high support to motivate high levels of performance; in these cases, it is impossible not to notice whether someone is doing great work or bad work. Because people in these cultures know that improvement is tough going and that disagreement is a normal part of any change, they are more inclined and prepared to confront opportunities for growth. Students, parents, and colleagues know when bad teaching is being tolerated (Fullan, 2005).

A propensity for teachers to inflate grades linked to their students' achievement is a significant issue (Dueck, 2014; Phelps, 2003). Teachers spend all of their time coaching students on ways to succeed and to reach their potential; then we ask them to assume the mantle of an evaluator who will assess the degree to which learning is achieved. Consequently, significant levels of *grade inflation* occur, and the whole process of having teachers acting as the *sole evaluator* of their own students is called into question. This is one of the reasons the educational system must incorporate *large-scale assessment and then evaluate the empirical evidence.*

Teaching is a relational activity, and being the conveyor of bad news is difficult and can stress the relationship. Informing students that they are failing to attain grade-level standards and that repeating a course would be in their best interests is difficult. The policy of social promotion—or passing failing students to the next class so they could remain with their peer group throughout their schooling—alleviated this discomfort and enabled the school *to avoid being held accountable for student achievement* and for the emotional trauma of separating students out from an age-peer group, even though such a separation would have meant the struggling student would have been kept with a group functioning at a similar stage in their learning.

Relationships interfere with objectivity. Society, in general, understands this reality and sets up criteria to take this into account. For example, obtaining a driver's license is a significant milestone on the path to adulthood. Parents are often involved in coaching their children to become good drivers. Accountability is high, because the parent is obviously concerned about the safety of their child; but parents are also concerned about the possibility of damage to their vehicle and the potential impact this will have on their insurance coverage. And so motivation to provide good coaching is at a high level, and many parents wisely reach out to others, such as a driver-training instructor, for assistance.

Our governments do not accept that a parent's heightened sense of accountability and motivation to ensure their son or daughter learns to drive well is sufficient to entrusting them with the responsibility to determine whether or not their child is ready for a driver's license. On the contrary, qualifying for a driver's license requires passing a standardized test as well as passing a test of practical road experience with an examiner, who makes the final determination about the new driver's readiness. A passing certificate, or driver's license, is only granted when potentially biased interpersonal relationships are removed from the skill evaluation. Even driver trainers who have served as coaches to the student drivers are considered too close to the student to give the final verdict.

In professional sports, the usual model in managing teams is to separate the coaching role from the team-selection process. Coaches manage the team in the sense of determining who will play what position and which players will be on the field of play at a given point in time. Between games they instruct players on how they can perform more effectively and use a variety of strategies to maximize the player's motivation.

However, someone with a higher level of responsibility and a greater sense of objectivity decides who can wear the team uniform in the first place. General managers coordinate player selection and deselection processes, including trades. These processes undoubtedly incorporate coaches' opinions, but the general manager is responsible for providing the team's coach or manager with the best player talent given the resources available. The general manager is also responsible to the team's president or owner for managing the coaches so performance throughout the organization is maximized.

In some areas of the private sector, the roles of coach and evaluator are conflated, but this is normal because the bottom line—or profit—acts as an independent *arbiter of performance*. There is a far more discernible bottom line where profit and loss are the significant measures. An owner is compelled to move quickly when employees are not doing their jobs efficiently and effectively. Underperformance in the private sector has the capacity to imperil the entire operation, so accountability is relatively simple and straightforward.

Teachers and school administrators, along with most other public employees, have been successful at resisting this model of accountability. *Educators focus more on process than on student outcomes, especially those related to academic achievement.* Too frequently educators look to blame the home for ineffective parenting or to government for providing insufficient funding. Blame is assigned to the student for a lack of motivation rather than to a teacher's lack of effort and talent.

A lack of bottom-line-measurement data related to student outcomes reduce principals to *measuring the processes teachers use in their classrooms*. Principals measure these processes against their own standards for how well these processes ought to be applied, but their judgments are clouded by their own philosophy regarding which teacher practices are the most suitable for student success. Within all of this activity, as well intentioned as it may be, there is a greater personal problem that principals must overcome.

While fulfilling their *coaching role*, principals have to build trust with teachers by forging strong relationships. Like teachers assessing their own students, principals assessing their own teachers believe they have been excellent coaches and that their teachers are thus well prepared for the evaluation. Recognizing shortcomings in their teachers' abilities can be interpreted as proving their coaching efforts were not effective. Not surprisingly, principals see some scant evidence of effective teaching and inflate the degree to which the teacher actually can apply it consistently.

PRINCIPALS' ROLE IN EVALUATING TEACHERS

Senior leadership in school districts have big-picture issues to resolve with few more critical than identifying the process for evaluating staff. Teachers are the backbone of the education system because students rely on their expertise to develop the skills, knowledge, and understanding necessary for pursuing a successful career. The key question is whether all teachers are equal as suggested by a reward system that mostly ignores quality of service.

Determining whether all teachers were equally talented was a quandary I faced as a first-year superintendent. My predecessor had saddled the school district with a negotiated clause that a qualified teacher on the substitute list would have to be hired before considering someone from outside. In other words, any teacher passing the bar of *minimal competence* would be given the position as long as they were experienced in the position.

Despite receiving more than 6,000 applications from the around the world to fill an open position, hiring from a pool of teachers passed over by the four surrounding districts unencumbered by this contractual requirement was an inhibitor to excellence. Selecting the best teacher from this small pool of possible candidates was also denied because seniority identified who would be awarded the contract. Frequently, a teacher hiring lasts for thirty-five years, and pursuing the best candidate can have a significant impact on the lives of hundreds of students.

The school board's first directive for me as the newly appointed superintendent was that I overturn this hiring requirement. But once a horse is out of the barn, recapture is a lot more complicated. Similarly, overturning the teachers' union's triumph was highly unlikely, and therefore a strategy to deflect this existing clause during the upcoming negotiations was chosen—but only after all of the contractual issues had been resolved. Serious bargaining commenced when only the offending clause remained.

The ensuing strike over this one clause lasted fifteen days before a small change was achieved. Specifically, a teacher from the substitute pool would have to produce two consecutive satisfactory reports on a list of seventeen elements of their teaching to be evaluated, with at least fourteen rated satisfactory. The bar was not raised very high, but hiring required an assessment of classroom performance in two assignments of more than three days. This minor shift ended the bitter dispute.

The next step provided a similarly daunting challenge. Teacher and administrator evaluations in the region utilized a five-point scale, with four ratings in the satisfactory range. During a period of several years, only one teacher's evaluation received the bottom rating of *less than satisfactory*. Expecting school principals to withstand the pressure against assessing unsatisfactory performance was a giant leap for the school district, because the degree of separation in schools from unionized teachers was nonexistent. Schools function best when collegial relationships prevail, and they would not prevail if principals handed out unsatisfactory ratings.

The process for evaluating principals during those years included staff input, with minimal emphasis on student outcomes. Assessing student outcomes was in its infancy and too imprecise for use in evaluating staff. Principals understood the simple principle of mutual backscratching and how their performance review might be influenced by the viewpoints of staff. The minor gains we had achieved in bargaining for proof of greater competency among the substitute-teacher pool applying for a permanent teacher position could be entirely negated if a principal, thinking of their own evaluation, also worried about preserving the good opinion of the teachers who evaluated them. A principal might be unwilling to be frank about which candidates were weak because the odds of having a specific candidate placed in his/her school was minimal.

Inserting an additional filter was necessary to ensure that a hiring standard was based on a consistent assessment of quality. Therefore, principals always conducted the initial evaluation of an aspiring teacher on the substitute list—which, in virtually every instance, meant the principal awarded a positive evaluation. When the aspirant was in a long-term substitute-teacher assignment for the second time, a district principal conducted the critical second evaluation.

An individual not attached to the school evaluated applicants, using *common standards* meant to determine whether a teacher was competent in the seventeen teaching elements under evaluation—and which, therefore, ensured the candidate would only be hired to a position aligned with their training, like grade level or subject area. Recall that only fourteen of the assessed skill areas needed an acceptable rating. This second step with an evaluator external to the school frequently produced a significantly different result from the applicant's initial assessment, and, when insufficient satisfactory assessments occurred, aspirant teachers were required to begin the process anew.

This reminds us that well-intentioned school principals are in an untenable position that can significantly degrade their school's effectiveness. On the one hand, they are required to lead through influence and trust, while on the other they are to assess and evaluate in ways that could end a colleague's career. Is it realistic to think that a person can cultivate friendship and support one day while confronting mediocrity the next?

Coaching, a fundamental responsibility assigned to principals, requires a relationship of integrity developed over time, but can this bond be cultivated when both parties *know assessment devoid of personal feeling is also required?* Devoting a chapter to this issue is necessary, because it is *unrealistic to expect principals to play both roles*, and by insisting on it we have opted for an approach that ultimately *tolerates bad teaching.* A model of principals evaluating their own teachers is an example of teachers rather than students being atop education's pyramidal pinnacle.

THE BACK-SCRATCH EFFECT

The entire teacher-supervision process is tainted by a wrong-headed focus on how the principal is evaluated by the very same people under evaluation—namely, teachers. In essence, this approach is characterized by a culture of I'll-scratch-your-back-if-you-scratch-mine. This conflict of interest should, by itself, be sufficient to end the practice *unless the educational system incorporates a check-and-balance approach, with a principal-evaluation model that focuses primarily on student outcomes in the school.*

Such a model, where coaches evaluate their direct reports, is also an issue in school-district offices. One superintendent commented that she followed a five-level-scale evaluation model for her assistant superintendents. It was the first occasion when empirical-data sources gleaned from client-satisfaction surveys were used in staff evaluations within the district. These evaluations were not just a pass/fail model but also utilized the five-level-scale, ranging from *excellent* to *less than satisfactory*.

Based on the data as well as her observations, this superintendent identified several areas with each subordinate where work performance was solid but did not demonstrate excellence. On this basis, the overall performance was rated *very good*. These assistant superintendents were displeased that their evaluations left some ratings below *excellent*. It was standard practice in surrounding districts to evaluate senior staff as excellent, and these specific senior staff worried that a rating less than the perceived norm could negatively impact their career opportunities.

In essence, senior staff believed an excellent performance rating was their *entitlement. The politically correct action was to provide the norm.* Introducing empirical data made it impossible for evaluators to come to a conclusion where everyone is assessed to be excellent, because the data differentiated employees' ratings on the basis of performance. This superintendent blazed a trail of nonconformity, and she would pay the price. Those who were disgruntled with her objective evaluation formed a small alliance and waited until it was their turn to evaluate her and settle the score.

At the school level, *the problem is that principals provide high ratings for their teachers because teachers will rate them when their leadership will be evaluated by district leaders*. This pattern of behavior is replicated further up the hierarchy as assistant superintendents want high evaluations from their principals when the superintendent is conducting their performance reviews. Similarly, the superintendent is anticipating loyalty from underlings when the school board is reviewing their leadership. Everyone is looking to have their own back scratched. Once again, standards suffer because performance levels are inflated.

The proof of how ineffective the current evaluation process for educators can be is found in the deselection data. The current model is not weeding out ineffective teachers, because standards are too low. Principals are not calling a spade a spade. The educational system places too much emphasis on staff relationships to the detriment of student outcomes. In the area of teacher supervision, *the educational system is once again arranged in a way that not only falls short of the student's best interest but is also arranged in a way that runs counter to the student's best interest.*

This unfortunate reality, *where relationships blind objectivity*, supports the union's primary objective, which is to look after the welfare of their members. They are not committed to looking after the best interests of the system's clients by ridding classrooms of ineffective practitioners. Neither are they supportive of using large-scale testing programs to identify weak teachers who may need to feel some pressure to improve. *Unions cannot pursue simultaneously the best interests of their members and the system's clients.* Their conflict of interest is self-evident.

This is depressingly easy to illustrate. One superintendent spoke of his experience with the union at the negotiating table. The union's position was that all teachers are excellent but that *management is to blame for the poor level of service from some because teachers were not placed properly where they can excel.* The teacher might function more effectively if there were fewer students in the class or if there were fewer students demonstrating special needs. The union's perspective was that the superintendent was not making sufficient effort to place the teacher in situations where their capacity for excellence could be displayed.

Why are state politicians so complacent about this clearly inadequate system of staff supervision? One of the most obvious reasons is that their governance structure also operates without adequate concern for the bottom line. Public-sector enterprises share a common ethos, and politicians looking to right the ship in education would have to right their own first. In other words, they would have to tackle the self-centeredness of their own government's unions first and then deal directly with the ensuing conflict.

Well-intentioned incompetence is a major issue imperiling our society. Courage is a virtue we want all politicians to demonstrate, but it is a rare virtue, particularly when a politician's careers is always at stake. This explains their propensity to spend on projects those who elected them favor, and it explains why they are reticent to deal with complex and nebulous issues like staff supervision in schools, even though they might personally consider it an issue worthy of their attention.

School-district officials associated with educational leadership are fairly knowledgeable about superintendent Michelle Rhee's efforts to "weed-out" poor teachers in Washington, D.C., in the late 2000s. She was known for her ability to remove poor teachers! In the end, the political heat her employers experienced was beyond their ability to endure. Having to choose between policies that championed students and those that favored interest groups, the school board waivered and then capitulated. Rhee went on to other educational endeavors.

Rhee was successful on least at one level: she used empirical evidence to show how bad the situation was and who the weak teachers were. *A critical point presented in this chapter is that coaches cannot evaluate unless they use empirical data to influence the evaluation process.* Data provides the basis for differentiated evaluations and the *likelihood of tension in working relationships.*

For principals to serve as effective team evaluators, they have to resort to empirical evidence, which is best for students in any case. Any other method of evaluation will lead to dysfunction. Even a simple statement that appears to have a negative connotation may produce conflict or even sever a relationship. Once the relationship is damaged, the principal will surely experience difficulty when it comes time for their assessment from the district office. The solution is to introduce higher levels of objectivity into the process.

REVEALING THE HIDDEN SECRETS OF A POOR EVALUATION SYSTEM

The media is now beginning to educate the public and provide for much greater transparency in the school system so that an informed public can influence developments in the school. *Waiting for "Superman,"* a proeducation reform documentary, indicated that one out of every fifty-seven doctors loses their license to practice medicine, one out of every ninety-seven lawyers loses their license to practice law, and in many major cities, only one out of 1,000 teachers is fired for performance-related reasons (Chilcott & Guggenheim, 2010).

Newspaper reporters are now investigating the issue, and their findings are summarized by the Center for Union Facts (Dueck, 2014):

- The *New York Daily News* reports that "over the past three years [2007–2010], just 88 out of some 80,000 (New York) city schoolteachers have lost their jobs for poor performance." (Approximately 0.1 percent)
- The *Albany Times Union* looked at what was going on outside New York City and discovered that of 132,000 teachers; only 32 were fired for any reason between 2006 and 2011. (Approximately 0.02 percent)
- In Chicago, *Newsweek* reported that only 0.1 percent of teachers were dismissed for performance-related reasons between 2005 and 2008. In a school district that has by any measure failed its students—only 28.5 percent of 11th graders met or exceeded expectations on that state's standardized tests. [The problem is worse than it seems because there are two Chicago's: north and south. In the north neighborhoods like Lincoln Park are found some of the highest performing schools. So how bad are the schools in the south? The averages make Chicago look bad, but the bad is far worse than the average]
- The *Los Angeles Times* in 2009 reported that, in a school district where the graduation rate in 2003 was just 51 percent, between 1995 and 2005, only 112 Los Angeles tenured teachers faced termination—eleven per year— out of 43,000. (Approximately 0.03 percent annually)
- In ten years, only about 47 out of 100,000 teachers were actually terminated from New Jersey's schools. (Approximately 0.05 percent over 10 years)
- In any given year in Florida, scholar Richard Kahlenberg wrote, the involuntary dismissal rate for teachers was an abysmally low 0.05 percent, "compared with 7.9 percent in the Florida workforce as a whole."

- In Dallas, even when unofficial pressures to resign are factored in, only 0.78 percent of tenured teachers are terminated.
- Out of Tucson, Arizona's 2,300 tenured teachers, only seven have been fired for classroom behavior in the past five years. (Approximately 0.3 percent over 5 years)
- Des Moines, Iowa a school district with almost 3,000 teachers has fired just two for poor performance in five years. (Approximately 0.07 percent over 5 years)

Anderson (2013), a writer for the *New York Times*, reported that roughly 100 percent of teachers in Florida were deemed effective or highly effective in recent evaluations. Incredibly, teacher evaluations in 2011 typically involved a *single observation of about 20 minutes*. In Tennessee, 98 percent of teachers were judged to be *at expectations*. In Michigan, 98 percent of teachers were rated effective or better. An official with the National Council on Teacher Quality conceded in an interview that "there are some alarm bells going off . . . There's a real culture shift that has to occur, and there's a lot of evidence that hasn't occurred yet."

What is the cultural shift that must happen? Even though some teacher evaluations are partly contingent on student test scores, evaluations are mostly focused on principals' assessments acquired through their own observations of the teachers. There is a need to abandon a culture where almost all teachers are considered *above average*.

Anderson (2013) points out how this problem of low standards is exacerbated by the involvement of evaluators "who generally are not detached managerial types and can be loath to give teachers low marks." Education is strengthened by having relational people working with students: it is weakened by requiring these well-intentioned people to "bell the cat" of mediocre colleagues. This emphasis on relationships is why there is not a substantial increase in the percentage of teachers who are removed from the classroom. This may also be why Florida's principals wrote their teachers' evaluations based on one twenty-minute observation.

When Anderson (2013) informed Grover J. Whitehurst, director of the Brown Center on Education Policy at the Brookings Institution, that very few teachers were deemed "ineffective," Whitehurst responded, "It would be an unusual profession that at least 5 percent are not deemed ineffective." Evaluating and developing talent is the most important management function in the educational system, whether it is occurring in the classroom with students by their teachers or with teachers by their principals. However, *low standards are endemic in the educational system*, even though we claim that education is vital to our nation's future well-being.

Mellon (2010) explores the problem of low standards and asks why, in the past, teachers have rarely been let go because of poor classroom performance. In an interview with Houston's superintendent, Terry Grier, who has run nine school districts over twenty-five years, Grier theorizes, "I think some principals accept mediocrity because they don't want to go through the battle with the teachers' union or through the process of aggressively recruiting others." *There is a need to apply pressure on those who lack the courage to combat mediocrity.*

The idea of applying *pressure* is emotionally charged within education. Fullan (2009) expands our thinking about the value of using pressure to motivate activity, writing, "The opposite of pressure is not no pressure. No pressure is complacency. No pressure is inertia's other best friend" (p. 122). Fullan continues,

> A focused sense of urgency gets people's attention; partnership and peer learning increase support but also pressure from successful cases (if it is done in circumstances similar to ours); transparency of data makes it even more evident who is successful and who is not. (p. 126)

Fullan explains the differences between positive and negative pressure, making the critical point that pressure is not an either/or situation. Pressure can be very motivational and is enhanced by transparency: "It exposes not only results but practices that produce results. It generates specific, precise, visually clear images of what works. It is accessible for all as it takes all excuses off the table" (p. 123).

Incorporating objective data, such as student achievement on tests, applies additional pressure to raise teaching standards, but this method of teacher evaluation is not without its own hiccups. Such an evaluator framework is still managed by people within the system and so can still be politically manipulated, as evidenced by Anderson's (2013) report on one U.S. county. Teacher evaluations were relatively stringent, establishing *cut scores*, using students' test data, but when only 78 percent of teachers were deemed highly effective or effective, and when they saw how lenient other neighboring districts in the county were, they reset their standards much lower. Ultimately, 99.4 percent of teachers in this county were rated effective or highly effective.

A NEW FRONTIER IN TEACHER EVALUATION

Utilizing test scores in teacher-evaluation systems is a relatively new endeavor. There will be problems not unlike those evident in how teachers assess students. *Misuse by some does not mean we should disuse generally.* There is more promise for fairness incorporating student test data into teacher evaluations than when educational systems rely exclusively on the teachers' own assessments of their students' work in the classroom. The significant degree of grade inflation that occurs when a teacher-student relationship influences assessment is a concern.

Many school systems rely on external tests for generating marks used in decisions regarding scholarships and placements into prestigious universities. This methodology requires a consistent application of cut scores so that there is adherence to standards and it is ensured that goal posts are not moving. Students may feel disadvantaged by not being able to influence marks through strategies like compliant behavior, but they benefit from having their learning assessed by an unbiased process. *Fairness to students* is enhanced.

Undoubtedly teacher unions will continue to denounce the use of test scores in evaluating teachers. Introducing measures of empirical data decreases their opportunity to challenge ratings of poor performance in the classroom. Even though teaching processes observed by evaluators continue to comprise most of the evaluation, there finally is a shift underway to consider learner outcomes. *Learning is no longer the sole responsibility of the student*. This shift, by itself, is a major revolution in education.

However, this revolution presents a problem for politicians. Their electability is threatened when they adopt an allegiance to students, *who cannot vote*. In New York State, for example, complaints quickly surfaced in 2014 when results from the new Common Core tests were released: 26 percent of students in 3rd through 8th grade passed the tests in English, and 30 percent passed in mathematics. These new tests emphasized deep analysis and creative problem-solving rather than the traditional testing approach that relies on short answers and memorization. In the previous year, when the old tests had been used, 47 percent of city students had passed in English and 60 percent in mathematics.

Across the state, the downward shift was similar: overall, 31 percent of New York students passed the exams in reading and mathematics compared with 55 percent in reading and 65 percent in mathematics the previous year. These poor results were chilling news for politicians, who quickly sanctioned the previous testing program where standards were being systematically reduced in order to qualify for improvement grants under No Child Left Behind legislation.

Their deception exposed, politicians reacted immediately as leaders of both political parties in the New York State Legislature called on the state to back away from plans to use those exams to grade teacher performance. A news report in the *New York Times* on February 4, 2014, captured the political paranoia:

> In synchronized statements, Democratic leaders of the State Assembly joined Republicans in the State Senate to propose that the tests, which are aligned with the new curriculum standards known as the Common Core, be excluded,

for now, from the state's new teacher evaluation system, which Gov. Andrew M. Cuomo signed into law in 2012.

The proposal will involve altering the law, which requires that the state test results be used for at least 20 percent of a teacher's evaluation. Other factors, like principals' observations and locally designed tests, make up the bulk of the grade. Teachers who earn the lowest mark—"ineffective"—two years in a row are at risk of losing their jobs.

The change would require backtracking on one of the governor's earliest legislative victories. But it also could give him an antidote to mounting complaints over the Common Core in a reelection year. Mr. Cuomo has already said he would name a panel to recommend changes to what he called a "flawed" rollout of the Common Core. (Baker, 2014)

The key phrase in this article—*an antidote to mounting complaints over the Common Core in a reelection year*—demonstrates succinctly how *politicians perpetuate unfairness to their students in deference to teachers and their unions*. Too frequently, elections precipitate politicians' subjugating education's clients' best interests simply because they are not on the voters' lists. For a period of time, the New York school system will revert to an evaluation system based on principals' evaluations, as deeply flawed as this process is.

This hesitation to proceed with the most challenging aspect of attaching consequences with performance as required in the United States' Race to the Top initiative provides a clear example regarding how politicians align with their most powerful special interest group: teachers' unions. New York is a Democratic state, and teacher's unions support Democratic candidates overwhelmingly. OpenSecrets.org reports that

> Based on required filings with the federal government, it is estimated that between 1990 and 2002, 80 percent of the NEA's substantial political contributions went to Democratic Party candidates. Although this has been questioned as being out of balance with the more diverse political views of the broader membership, the NEA maintains that it bases support for candidates primarily on the organization's interpretation of candidates' support for public education and educators. Every presidential candidate endorsed by NEA must be approved by majority vote among the members themselves at NEA's annual Representative Assembly. (Dueck, 2014)

Similar delays in incorporating student achievement on system tests into teacher evaluations are reported in 2014 for California and Iowa. Both states voted Democrat in the 2012 presidential election. *It is not an overstatement to say that the power of teachers' unions is persuasive and pervasive.*

Nevertheless, progress in attaching higher levels of accountability to teachers for improving student achievement is being made across the United States. One publication put out by The National Council on Teacher Quality

(Dueck, 2014), reports a successful trend using data for the years 2009, 2011, and 2013, which evaluates the criteria states use for the evaluation of quality in education:

- Requiring annual evaluation of all teachers: 15, 25, and 28 states
- Student achievement is the preponderant criterion in teacher evaluation: 4, 13, and 20 states
- And evidence of effectiveness is the basis of teacher tenure decisions: 0, 8, and 19 states.

Making use of empirical data is a critical aspect for creating valid and reliable teacher evaluations; however, there remains a requirement to resolve the issue that coaches should not also be the evaluator. School administrators wanting to achieve the highest level of teamwork possible risk many negative consequences when they provide staff with multilevel evaluations (that is, five-point-scale evaluations), including risking severing the relationship.

Edmonton school district in Alberta was once identified as the best school district in North America because it pioneered school-based decision-making and magnet schools. Its success was also heralded for improving student achievement the longer the student was enrolled within the district. A follow-up conversation with the superintendent revealed his commitment to instructional leadership. During his four-year tenure, 7,500 classrooms were visited after discussions with the principal, whom he asked three basic questions: What will we see? What won't we see? What is your coaching plan for this teacher?

A school district with 80,000 students can easily extract central-office staff from their instructional leadership functions by making administrivia their primary mandate. These visits from the superintendent consumed a significant amount of time, but ensuring that schools were improving was this superintendent's central purpose. His slogan, "Failure is not an option," was a driving force and, *when a school was not improving, this superintendent intervened in the school's autonomy by designing the school's professional-development program.*

Parents were the beneficiaries of this passionate leadership, *because their children were winning.* Some people may espouse that a politically correct posture is to have school staff prepare their professional development so that ownership is enhanced. Instead this superintendent believed there is a sense of urgency to make sure some students are not disadvantaged only in the name of accommodating political correctness. Years later on March 1, 2010, U.S. president Barack Obama made a related statement to the U.S. Chamber of Commerce. He said, "Our kids only get one chance at an education, and we need to get it right" (Zeleny, 2010).

Principals may be well-intentioned people, but their track record in evaluating teachers is abysmal. Mutually beneficial back-scratching dominates our schools' politically correct culture, where people other than students occupy a pyramidal pinnacle. Teacher evaluation is so important that it must be the focus of all administrators selected for leadership functions in school-district offices. Achieving excellent teacher services for our children requires a two-pronged approach: the principal's work should be focused on *developing teacher talent*, while the district office is responsible for providing an arms-length function of *evaluating teacher performance.*

This book's focus is on employing strategies for effective service at several levels of educational leadership. This chapter reveals how current standards in teacher evaluations are too low, demonstrating why this concern must be addressed to provide a fairer and more honest appraisal approach. Inflated performance evaluations are related to students' grade inflation, and the superintendent is the key decision maker for ensuring realistic assessments for both students and staff. Hence our need to incorporate comprehensive analysis of data surrounding both issues.

Chapter Eleven

Provincial and State Leadership

We have stated that as the teacher goes, so goes the class, that as the principal goes, so goes the school, and that as the superintendent goes, so goes the district. Now our attention is focused on provincial or state leadership and how this level of direction can make a difference in schools. The bottom line is that all leadership makes a difference, but the significant question is whether the difference is *positive* or *negative*. Seldom do we describe the potential for leadership contributing negatively to our quality of life or service. To do so would simply be politically incorrect; yet it is a reality that not all leadership is good leadership.

School-system leadership in North America resides with states and provinces and is focused mostly on government policy. In other countries, the federal office of education articulates national policy that is administered at the regional level. In Canada and the United States, however, educational policy is more decentralized to the regions and administered in local school districts. Therefore the province or state establishes the highest level of direction, and educational administrators reporting to these elected officials advise on the overall policies guiding their region.

Reporting to these politicians requires extensive review of regional data accompanied with thoughtful, logical reasoning for maintaining or revising existing policy. Working in this political shadow also demands a commitment to speaking *truth to power* based on what is in students' best interests, while providing bang for the taxpayers' buck. It is less important for a regional politician to maintain their popularity with constituents than it is for superintendents within school districts, because the regional politician is more mindful of demonstrating how policies have improved government outcomes.

Chapter 7, therefore, provides critical information for district and school leaders regarding the widespread inconsistency demonstrated in teachers assessing student achievement. In Alberta, five ministers of education believed this data provided irrefutable evidence for supporting the ongoing need for standardized testing. Trustee and parent organizations also voiced their support for standardized testing, which remains the mainstay of Alberta's Accountability Pillar—a government-created system of measuring the school system's success and progress.

The need for an effective gauge of educational success led the province to construct a test so proficient that it earned a statement from a U.S. Department of Education official, who wrote, "You have built in Alberta what we want across the United States." This sentiment launched the U.S .Race to the Top initiative, with its emphasis on Common Core, which is another way of saying common *standards* have been created for all students in U.S. publicly funded schools.

LEADERSHIP: POSITIVE OR NEGATIVE

Notwithstanding the fact that large-scale testing has become a political flash point, its ongoing use has the potential to improve student learning. Several international tests provide valuable information about student achievement:

- The Trends in International Mathematics and Science Study (TIMSS) is a test assessing the mathematics and science learning of students in grades 4 and 8.
- The Progress in International Reading Literacy Study (PIRLS) is a test assessing reading comprehension in students in grade 4.
- And the Programme for International Student Assessment (PISA) is a test for fifteen-year-old students that assesses learning in science, mathematics, and reading to gauge an education system's overall effectiveness.

Many countries, states, and provinces have developed their own large-scale testing programs that are similar to the international tests and useful for improving student achievement.

Michael Fullan, a highly acclaimed international education consultant and researcher from Canada, expresses the value of testing for student achievement:

> A by-product of external accountability, assessment for learning refers to "any assessment for which the first priority is to serve the purpose of promoting students' learning.". . . Even using external tests as the criterion, . . . [improvements have been] documented . . . in the results of most teachers, which, "If replicated across the whole school . . . would raise the performance of a school

at the 25th percentile of achievement nationally into the upper half." (Fullan, 2005, p. 54, quoting Black et al., 2003, pp. 2, 29)

Simply stated, standardized testing, *when understood as administering the same test across many classrooms*, has the capacity to improve student achievement. Utilizing this strategy is an example of positive leadership.

Douglas Reeves, another well-respected leader in educational research from the United States, gave a presentation in Los Vegas at an educators' conference on assessment in 2007. There he stated the value of common assessments:

> When . . . I note that all schools with gains of more than 20 percent in student achievement also happen to employ common assessments, extensive nonfiction writing, and collaborative scoring by the faculty, then I can begin to draw inferences that common assessments, nonfiction writing, and collaborative scoring are at the very least associated with improved student performance. (Reeves, 2004, p. 54)

Reeves is another powerful voice in the field of education calling for the use of standardized testing in order to improve student learning.

John Bishop studied the effects of high school examinations in New York and concluded that

> Thirty percent of American teachers say they "feel pressure to give higher grades than students' work deserves." Thirty percent also feel pressured "to reduce the difficulty and amount of work you assign." . . .
>
> Under a system of external exams, teachers and local school administrators lose the option of lowering standards to reduce failure rates and raise self-esteem. The only response open to them is to demand more of their students so as to maximize their chances of being successful on the external exams. (Bishop, 2002, quoting Peter D. Hart Research Associates, 1995)

Bishop presents a powerful argument regarding the potential to reduce the tendency to inflate grades, which is so prevalent in our schools.

Bishop summarized the results of the TIMSS as pointing to the benefit of standardized tests for students:

> Our review of the evidence suggests that the claims by advocates of standards based reform that curriculum-based external exit examinations significantly increase student achievement are probably correct. Students from countries with such systems outperform students from other countries at a comparable level of economic development by 1.3 grade equivalents in science and 1.0 grade equivalents in mathematics. (Bishop, 1997, p. 18)

In Canada, all ten provinces participate in PISA every three years when the assessment is given. Oversampling occurs within each province so that student results can be treated the same as national results. Canada's educational system is unique because it is the only country in the developed world without a national office of education. Therefore its standardized-testing results are reported nationally as well as provincially.

Alberta has employed testing for all students in grades 3, 6, and 9 since 1995 and for grade 12 for more than a century. Its students performed at the highest or second-highest level among Canadian provinces on all three components (reading, mathematics, and science) in four PISA tests in 2000, 2003, 2006, and 2009. Alberta's overall performance in 2003 was also at the highest level for any of the nations (and provinces) involved in PISA.

Manitoba began provincial testing at the same time as Alberta and ranked fourth overall among the ten provinces in PISA 2000. In 1999, an election promise to Manitoba's teachers to do away with compulsory testing precipitated a change in government. By the time their grade 3 students reached the age of fifteen and wrote the PISA 2009, this province's performance dropped to an overall Canadian ranking of ninth out of ten provinces. By not having provincial testing serve to check and balance accountability, students in this province experienced a significant educational setback. In plain and simple language, the government failed its students and provided poor educational leadership for the province.

Meanwhile, Ontario ranked fifth overall in PISA 2000 when their provincial-testing program began with assessments in reading and mathematics in grades 3, 6, and 9. Student achievement relative to the other provinces improved to an overall third-place ranking in PISA 2009. In this instance, government leadership achieved greater levels of student success because it implemented provincial testing as a check and balance to accountability.

By 2013, amazing success was seen within a Canadian jurisdiction that had habitually been known to have the lowest levels of student achievement. Students' class marks had always been high in this jurisdiction because standards employed by teachers had been so low. Grade inflation had hidden the problems from citizens until common assessments across the country prodded the province's political arm into using common assessments across the province.

In the 2013 Canada-wide reading assessment, Prince Edward Island moved upward to a sixth-place ranking of the ten provinces. Coincidentally, Manitoba, as predicted when they did away with standardized testing, dropped into last place, while Ontario moved into first. In mathematics, PEI students achieved a fourth-place ranking, while Manitoba placed a dismal last and Ontario placed second. In science, PEI placed sixth, while Manitoba was last and Ontario was second. Predictions made years earlier were borne out! PEI moved upward dramatically after incorporating common assessment, while Manitoba flopped after dropping these same assessments. Ontario's participation in common assessments also improved that province's rankings.

This Canadian data is noteworthy because it underscores the value for student achievement when common tests are utilized across the system. The trends evident reinforce the concept that *accountability is an investment, not an expense*. It is also noteworthy that the cost of each of Alberta's tests was less than $10 per student, which covered all elements of test preparation and marking. *A relatively small investment in accountability packs a powerful punch in improvement.* Large-scale assessment may be controversial among some stakeholders, but its benefit in improving student achievement is worth the investment.

There were also some results within Alberta's testing program that further demonstrated the positive impact of its testing program. This program of universal testing became fully operational in 1997 with the 1998–1999 school year, yielding a full set of results in language arts, mathematics, social studies, and science. Aggregated results for the next year—1999–2000—demonstrated a 5 percent improvement. This was followed by an additional improvement of 3 percent in 2000–2001, for a total aggregated improvement of 8 percent in the first two years after the initial year of testing.

Teachers felt pressure to teach all aspects of the curriculum—not only teach those they had chosen. In other words, more of the curriculum would be taught, and what was being covered would now be taught more effectively. In Alberta, the 8 percent improvement across the education system over the initial two years of using standardized testing proved a significant return in investment.

A follow-up conversation with Ontario education officials reported on a humorous situation in that province where teachers habitually taught about dinosaurs in virtually all classes and in every grade. Students enjoyed studying dinosaurs and were highly motivated. When, eventually, Toronto was awarded a professional basketball team, they named it the Raptors. When Ontario implemented system-wide testing, they, too, experienced immediate improved student achievement because teachers were teaching the entire curriculum in tested subjects.

Therefore supporting standardized testing is a critical initiative for system administrators; in Alberta's case, adopting standardized testing led to that province's appointment as national lead for the Pan-Canadian Assessment Program, which uses standardized testing to assess the nation's educational systems. These provincial experiences invite provincial comparisons that are not universally supported. For example, opponents claim a common and consistent approach to student assessment is a threat to education.

Chapter 11

STANDARDIZED TESTS VILIFIED INAPPROPRIATELY

Standardized tests are now perceived as the villain, because they are the messenger (Phelps, 2003). They measure individual student achievement and provide the basis for assessing the individual teacher's contribution to student achievement. For the first time in the history of education, teacher performance is quantifiable, and, while not negating entirely the use of subjective measurement criteria, this largely numerical approach to describing performance is creating significant anxiety among teachers. In a workforce considering job security a fundamental right, the idea that one could be demoted or even lose a job was almost unthinkable, even though it was the standard in much of the marketplace where teachers are served.

It is not surprising, then, that the possibility of assessing teacher performance based on student achievement as measured by standardized testing is attracting the overwhelming attention of teacher unions. Using standardized tests to measure student learning has always concerned unions, because they have understood that this carries with it the possibility of also measuring teacher quality. The National Education Association, the largest labor union in the United States, acknowledged this connection in a 2012 news release:

NEA President Says Misuse of Standardized Tests Must Stop

High-stakes decisions based on bad tests hurt students and educators
WASHINGTON—January 06, 2012—No Child Left Behind (NCLB) has been a major factor in the proliferation of poor quality standardized tests. As we celebrate the 10th anniversary of the flawed legislation and as Congress prepares to reauthorize the law, NEA is urging careful consideration of the fact that these tests are being used to make high-stakes decisions about students' and teachers' futures and have corrupted the pursuit of improving real learning and effective teaching.

"When we use shoddy, fill-in-the bubble tests as the basis for an accountability system—tests that frequently aren't aligned with what's being taught in classrooms—so-called accountability systems lose all credibility," said NEA President Dennis Van Roekel. "It doesn't make sense to students, educators, parents, or credible testing experts, and now they're fighting back."

"Well-designed assessment systems do have a critical role in student success. We should use assessments to help students evaluate their own strengths and needs, and help teachers improve their practice and provide extra help to the students who need it."

As Congress continues to consider the reauthorization of the Elementary and Secondary Education Act (ESEA) and as state legislatures prepare to consider more education legislation this year, Van Roekel emphasized that NEA "remains hopeful that policy makers will wake up from the standardized test craze" and change policies to reflect what research has consistently shown: no single measure of either student learning or teacher performance can ever be the sole determinant of success or failure. Van Roekel stressed that we need robust assessment systems, designed to help all students—systems that make sense to students, parents, educators, and communities.

"High-stakes standardized tests that are used to punish students, teachers and schools, make testing companies more money, but they don't make students any smarter. Only good teaching, good parenting and good study habits will help ensure student success," said Van Roekel. (National Education Association, 2012)

This union president made a significant statement when he says "no single measure of either student learning or teacher performance can ever be the sole determinant of success or failure." Until recently, teachers have been the sole determinants of student learning, yet we have seen how their capacity to provide accurate assessments is significantly flawed. Principals have been the sole determinants of teacher quality, and we have also seen how their conclusions are questionable. The primary point here is that the NEA is both acknowledging the need for an assessment of teachers and linking it to student assessment.

The NEA president also concluded his statement with a reference to standardized tests not making students any smarter. Teacher unions added their own statements of support to the NEA's stance, saying that "Just weighing a pig doesn't fatten it." This statement is designed to confuse the public into thinking that standardized tests are inconsequential and a waste of time. Aside from developing this absurd metaphor, the comparison denigrates the important work teachers do with children. Developing a child's mind to become a contributor in society should not be trivialized by comparing it to fattening a pig.

To a pig farmer, weighing the pig can be important when attempting to determine which ingredients produce the greatest gain. Once the formula is developed, it can be used repeatedly. A child's brain is different: A formulated process for each child is unknown. Testing provides the intelligence that good teachers can use for determining their success in developing each child's capacity. Assessment provides teachers with knowledge regarding where teaching is required and where practice may need change.

The significant issue in this debate centers on the concept of standardized testing. In simple terms, *standardized testing is any assessment given to two or more students*. With this understanding it is clearly evident that every teacher believes in standardized testing, because they use this approach on a regular basis. Routinely teachers use tests to assess their students' grasp of spelling and basic facts in mathematics. End-of-chapter and unit tests also qualify as standardized measurements in this simple definition of the concept, as do the myriad worksheets utilized in classrooms on a daily basis.

Many tests are constructed wholly or in part by individual teachers who spend an hour or two on their local "standardized" test and seldom draw on best-practice principles. Professional test makers, by way of contrast, spend considerable time surveying classrooms for quality test items, which are then field-tested, and the results carefully analyzed, before the test is given in a process that takes up to a year.

And so, strictly speaking, standardized testing is not the real *villain* as far as teachers are concerned; rather, it is the fact that these tests are given to *more than one class of students at the same time. Comparability* of results between students in different classrooms is creating a high level of anxiety now evident across the education system. Comparability is the teachers' villain!

Therefore it is now possible to compare teachers' success and, therefore, to differentiate salaries and legitimately reward teachers on the basis of quantified effectiveness. As far as unions are concerned, these *messengers* of student learning must be vilified; otherwise the union will find it more difficult to protect members who fail to meet the standard.

The NEA's president also uses an overstatement to confuse the issue. Can these standardized tests be one of several measures? Is a comprehensive examination of student achievement important in evaluating students and their teachers, school, and school district? The answer should be obvious, but the president implies that only one test is used to evaluate the teacher and so therefore standardized tests are inappropriate. If the system had actually been set up the way the NEA intimates that it is, it would be unfair for both students and teachers, but assessment is more complex than this. Statements like those of the president confuse and mislead the public.

"NARROWING THE CURRICULUM" IS A MEANINGLESS APPREHENSION

Teachers chafe at large-scale testing, claiming that tests "narrow the curriculum" and force them to "teach to the test." These slogans are intended to misguide the public and politicians, who may be too naive to understand the ramifications. There is one aspect of the narrowing-the-curriculum argument that may have some validity, but the criticism is misdirected. Phelps explains:

> Test critics commonly accuse high-stakes tests of "narrowing the curriculum," but it is actually the amount of time available that narrows it. In fact, all educators, including those opposed to standardized tests, narrow the curriculum. They have to. There is only so much instructional time available, and choices must be made as to how that time is used. It is physically impossible to teach everything that can be possibly taught. (Phelps, 2003, p. 42)

Education over the course of many decades added courses and content to school programs but avoided the difficult issue of negotiating contracts that would have extended students' learning time and teachers' work year. *It is not surprising that many students struggle with their basic skills in such a crowded curriculum, because politicians avoided dealing with the difficult labor issues.* The point is that teachers are narrowing the curriculum not because of large-scale testing but because there is *insufficient time for dealing with the basic skills* in the program of studies coupled with many additional programs—like technology, fine arts, health and safety, and so on.

State and national testing programs actually document the degree to which students are shortchanged in the basic education they receive. When teachers argue that their testing programs force them to narrow their instruction to basic skills, poor results on system tests demonstrate that a poor job is being done to ensure mastery of basic skills. Imagine what the results would be were teachers not concentrating on the basic skills deemed necessary for their students but not assessed on standardized tests.

The public should be thankful that the education system feels *pressure* to ensure that basic education is covered. Everyone should be focused on pursuing the goal of providing our children with sufficient time to cover basic education, as well as the plethora of content added to the curriculum since the time when we were an agrarian society. *We are unrealistic in thinking that today's students can be sufficiently prepared for tomorrow's world using time allocations established in yesteryear.*

This issue of insufficient time to adequately accommodate new curricular components is confounded by *our need to have all students achieve graduation requirements.* One school administrator recalls a graduation address in the 1960s in which graduates were congratulated on having received an education equivalent to that received among the top 5 percent in the world. Obviously, there were many underdeveloped places in the world where children did not even have access to education, but even in North America many students dropped out of school prior to graduation.

According to Education Week, U.S. graduation data indicates that completion rates peaked in 1969, with 77 percent of that high school class earning diplomas. This is the high point for students achieving graduation in the United States. By 2007, the national graduation rate had fallen to 69 percent. Many children are being left behind in our transition from an agrarian to a technological society (Molnar, 2013).

The problem in our educational system is that we are jamming so much into the curriculum that many students are unable to keep pace. Progressing to graduation rates of three-quarters and more of an entire population introduces a *significantly wider range of student abilities within our classrooms.* There are many students within this cohort requiring more than the hours currently provided in our schools to acquire the basic knowledge, skills, and attitudes required to live in our more complex world. Yet we expect that far less-capable students will experience success on par with students who find school relatively easy.

This unrealistic expectation of our less-capable students is the problem and a significant reason why educators feel they have to narrow the curriculum. In track events, for example, not everyone can run 100 meters in under ten seconds. Some will require twenty seconds or more to complete the journey, but they are not selected for Olympic tryouts. In school, not everyone can master today's updated and expanded curriculum in the 1,000 hours per year available to complete the educational journey. Of course teachers feel pressure to narrow the curriculum, and that narrowing is focused on what is being measured: the curriculum that society, through its political institutions, has judged and required by law to be the basic schooling required for an educated citizen.

This concern over narrowing the curriculum is also raised by educators suggesting that they are forsaking their responsibility to provide students with a well-rounded education, which includes subjects not assessed by large-scale tests. Some teachers say that they feel such pressure to teach only the basics in reading, writing, and mathematics in order for students to demonstrate sufficient skill acquisition that they do not have sufficient time to teach social studies, science, physical education, music, art, or any other number of subjects. Yet all of these courses are part of a curriculum derived from a legal process involving public decisions and not from an arbitrarily imposed or whimsically chosen roster of esoteric subjects.

In other words, it is the law to teach the set education program, and it is the prerogative of no single teacher to decide to ignore the responsibility to teach it. Of course teachers feel pressure, or accountability, to ensure that their students achieve basic skills necessary to succeeding in our society. Choosing to avoid their responsibility to teach other subject matter is a dereliction of duty that should be a matter of discipline. Of course, this would require that administrators monitor the degree to which teachers disregard their legal responsibilities.

This language may sound harsh to someone unfamiliar with the nuances of this debate. It is somewhat understandable that teachers might choose to concentrate on what is tested and measured. *The answer to this dilemma is not to do away with large-scale assessment but to expand it.* Every aspect of the curriculum should be assessed to ensure that students are taught the full program of studies—and that it is taught well.

With so much evidence demonstrating the value of large-scale assessment in improving student achievement, teacher unions should demand its greater use and thereby demonstrate their service orientation toward students. Instead of resisting administrators, they should be working with them to correct the problems that proper assessment reveals. When issues are identified in a normal cycle of standardized testing, they should exercise leadership that helps weak performers rather than excuses or shields them.

If unions are genuinely interested in student success, they should be clamoring to have large-scale assessment expanded to subjects not currently undergoing systematic assessment. There is too much evidence that teachers concentrate more on subjects where large-scale assessment occurs to the detriment of other subjects not so assessed—like art, physical education, and music. These programs are important and should be valued with the same expectations accorded to reading, writing, mathematics, social studies, and science.

One parent recorded observations he made about the performance of physical-education programs in his child's school. Few parents are permitted to observe teachers across their classes inside the school building. Parking his car outside of school playgrounds, and observing for quality of programs not included in the system's assessment program, this parent noted huge variations in the quality of instruction his child received. This experience helped him understand the value in using assessment as a tool for improving all aspects of schooling.

Given what we know today about accountability and assessment, teachers should be demanding that subjects not being currently tested, because they are difficult to assess with paper and pencil, be assessed in some other *standardized* way. It may be more costly, but group work, public speaking, and listening are skills that can and should be assessed, and the results could be used to improve instruction.

In other words, it is unconscionable that the school system, which knows what will help students, refuses to advocate for these changes because of self-interest. This is particularly distressing because it means that the system cannot help teachers who could be helped if there were openness and transparency. Elevating the importance of all subjects is a laudable objective.

Every student is entitled to learn the full curriculum, and learn it well. Every parent deserves to have their child provided with the skills, knowledge, and attitudes provided through exposure to the entire educational program. Taxpayers and their governments are entitled to have their investments provide all students with an education deemed necessary for living successfully. We want everyone to contribute to our society in a meaningful way. *It is an affront when educators choose to subvert their legal obligations by reducing their teaching in nontested programs because they want to look good in the areas measured by large-scale assessments.*

The foregoing is not promoting paper-and-pencil tests as the only means of assessing student learning. Assessments of student learning can occur when students demonstrate talent for teamwork, creativity, physical and musical ability, second language, speaking, and so on. While it is necessary to assess individual students in the basic curriculum, random samples can be applied in other areas. This procedure may be especially important during the introductory phase while we learn how to best assess these additional areas.

Skeptics might oppose efforts to increase assessment to all aspects of the curriculum because accountability could then be applied to all teachers in the school in addition to those teaching subjects currently being tested. Schools would experience productive pressure to ensure that all students receive a quality education in areas, including in some programs that teachers are teaching but in which they are not particularly talented.

"TEACHING TO THE TEST" IS ILL-CONCEIVED RHETORIC

The public's confusion regarding large-scale testing is also heightened by the educators' concern about "teaching to the test"—a fear just as misguided as fear over "narrowing the curriculum." It is absurd to test what is not taught. It is only fair to students that they be taught what is going to be tested. Vociferous and legitimate objections would be voiced if students were tested on content not contained within the curriculum.

In the period of time before states implemented large-scale testing programs, educators used generic tests from testing companies, which were not curriculum-specific. These generic tests were developed to accommodate the largest populated regions, such as the state of California in the United States and Canada's largest province, Ontario. Yes, most of the test items did fit the curriculum of other regions, but there were always some questions that were not a perfect match.

While teachers used these generic tests for their own purposes, they objected to any attempt to hold them accountable for the results because some questions did not relate to their state's curriculum. This proved to be a convenient dodge for any accountability and lead to today's testing programs, where states develop their own tests to match their curricula.

If teachers object to teaching to the test, what are they teaching? If the test is derived from the lawful curriculum, why protest? The reason why many states went through the arduous process of building curriculum frameworks in the 1990s was to ensure that all aspects of their curriculum were taught. Instructional omissions occurred because teachers were choosing to teach their *preferred* curriculum, sometimes to the exclusion of that mandated by the state. Instead of teaching *to* the test, should teachers teach *away* from the test?

Phelps provides a cogent description of the illogical situation taken by antitesting advocates:

> "Teaching to the test" is the perfect "damned if you do, damned if you don't" argument. Do not teach the material that will be covered in a test, and you will

be excoriated. Teach what will be covered in a test, and you will be excoriated. The only way out, of course, is the solution preferred by testing opponents—stop all testing (and let them run the schools the way they like). (Phelps, 2003, p. 40)

Tests expose lack of success. Tests reveal that there are differences in teacher quality. Tests demonstrate that some schools are more effective than others. Tests indicate that some students are disadvantaged by elements within their educational system. Tests make teachers, principals, system administrators, and politicians accountable for their leadership.

Standardized testing places pressure on these levels of leadership to employ meaningful improvement strategies. *They are our messengers of excellence and mediocrity*, which is the reason why some want them "killed." They are messengers that expose shortcomings and make the system feel uncomfortable—hence the name of Phelps's book, *Kill the Messenger*.

Teaching *to* the test is not the real issue. What is objectionable is when teachers *teach the test*. Some testing programs use the same tests for several administrations, and it is possible that some teachers access the questions unethically, using these actual questions for review in subsequent years before the questions are released for public use. This practice is cheating because it is *teaching the test*, literally.

This upside-down slogan, used by unions and educators, misrepresents aspects of assessment in an attempt to avoid accountability to provide students with an excellent education. They should be advocating that all aspects of the curriculum be assessed rather than not having any assessment. They should be promoting fairness to students by insisting that gains in student achievement be consistently and persistently monitored so that no one falls through the cracks. They should be advocating that schools provide more hours for instruction so that *pace of learning* can be accommodated.

Politicians' sympathetic ear to the incoherent arguments of antitesting proponents exposes their priorities. Rather than implementing testing programs that ensure greater fairness to students across the educational system, they placate educators seeking to absent themselves from accountability for student achievement. By casting their allegiance with the service providers, they demonstrate an attitude opposed to students' best interests.

Increasing student access to instructional time may make for messy negotiations, but today's living is more complex than yesterday's. Expecting every student to learn at the "superstar" rate is unrealistic. There are 8,760 hours in a year, and using only 1,000 of them, or less than 12 percent of the year, for education is insufficient and impractical for our nation's future well-being. Maintaining a teacher work year that supported our agrarian economy is no longer sufficient. Slavish adherence to old-fashioned organizational aspects of schooling is unconscionable.

Gaining and retaining power dominates the political arena. Politicians look to survive the next political test, which is an election some time within the next four years. Educators comprise a relatively large voting bloc of between 1 and 2 percent of the population and, since children are ineligible, a larger percentage of voters. Educators' votes can be the key to an election victory and holding political office.

There is a need for politicians to counter the snappy slogans craftily prepared to confuse the public. If they are unwilling to be the messengers of fact, *then they need to empower their bureaucrats to participate in the public debate.* These servants of the politicians have access to the information demonstrating how unfair the school system can be toward its students. Rather than pander to teachers for votes, politicians need to pander to the public for support by ensuring its education regarding how the nation's future is jeopardized.

In the United States, Common Core provides the means for comparing state results in student achievement so that some accountability or pressure is exerted to raise standards. Common assessment provides the measurement for ensuring that standards are achieved. Therefore, this assessment system is a relatively low-cost investment for demonstrating to the public that their investment in education is maximized. Comparability of results is not a wrong! Rather than attempting to kill the messenger, politicians should be focused on providing students with greater fairness, whether through more effective service from the education system or more reliable assessments from their teachers.

Chapter Twelve

Fully Enlisting Parents

Transferring power from the school system to parents provides the highest level of accountability in education and, therefore, parental involvement. A goal for fully enlisting parental involvement is a logical extension of efforts enunciated in earlier chapters before technology enabled school-level data collection. The advent of *quantitative* evidence now corroborates or refutes public perspectives based on *anecdotal* comments.

While I served as district superintendent, gathering objective information about each school was hallmark to my style of leadership. Test results using sample populations produced high-level discussions with principals regarding what really mattered: *student success*. These discussions were somewhat hampered because sample testing provided a convenient excuse when results were lower than expected. The potential for a majority of weaker students within the sample provided a convenient escape when discussing accountability for poor results.

Nevertheless, student achievement was finally assessed and tabulated for public review. Years later, the province accepted a recommendation to replace sample testing with universal assessment, which could be accurately reported on school-district report cards. Accountability for student achievement was rooted in the school system with opportunities to refine and enhance transparent evaluations of school performance.

Accountability was not only focused on student achievement. Satisfaction surveys from parents, students, and staff provided qualitative information regarding educational programs and staff service. Results from these surveys reinforced the theme that *accountability is an investment, not an expense*. Consistently over several years, survey results improved annually—a natural conclusion to publishing the data, which of course spurred a desire to improve through the district. The school district did not single out specific concerns for special attention; rather, increasing awareness motivated staff response.

These sets of information from testing and surveying were instrumental in diffusing tensions between parents and school principals. Occasions arose periodically when relationships grew strained, and some parents would energize a small group intent on dislodging a school administrator.

Some of these occasions necessitated administrative change because the quantitative information revealed deep-seated concerns. More frequently, however, the overall analysis provided evidence that the school was performing well and that the concern was localized to a specific situation or small group of malcontents. Displaying the information on the table sufficiently persuaded the distressed parties that resolving their issue would be best accomplished by working with the principal.

While objective information is a powerful tool in decision-making, not all groups perceive it as helpful to their cause. In one instance, annual surveys were initiated because of their influence in motivating positive change. Information provides a subtle incentive to refocus on areas evidencing lower levels of performance. In other words, some people feel pressure, and so they should!

Union leaders hear from membership's grumblers and take up their cause. Even when the annual results were demonstrating overall improvement, the local school board heeded the concerns from union heads, because many trustees relied on the unions' financial and verbal support during local elections.

The union solution proposed changing from an annual accountability program to one exercised every other year, despite the provincial government's public pronouncement that this school district had become its accountability model for education. Within three days of this board's decision to abandon annual surveys, I found myself a new career in accountability leadership within a different province. Pursuing accountability with a timid school board is professionally hazardous.

Publicly evaluating and communicating performance in education was and remains contentious. We have already demonstrated how standardized-test scores provide the most consistent assessment of student achievement. Ensuring public access to all assessment information instills motivation to improve, especially in areas where existing performance levels are poor.

Accountability is the critical piece in the puzzle for transferring power from educators to parents. Clear differences in performance levels are soon followed by expectations for choice, and these expectations are increasing. Unfortunately, students' transportation costs remain a final barrier for parents seeking to exercise choice.

DEMOCRATIZING EDUCATION

Educator's opposition to working in a competitive environment and transportation issues for parents are the significant obstacles for democratizing our school systems. Choice is a transformative benefit with few equals! Parents can shop and seek the most beneficial educational program for their child, which provides the stimulus for increasing their involvement in both the school as well as in their child's education. Educators also benefit from the increased motivation to excel in their performance because parents *choose* to place a child in their school.

Some readers may not appreciate comments regarding educator opposition to alternative-education programming within today's school system, such as private and charter schools. Many educators feel defensive about suggestions portraying their profession in a negative fashion, yet their leadership speaks on behalf of the profession. Presumably their comments and actions reflect the general position of members. Reckhow, Grossman, and Chung Evans summarized their perceptions regarding American teachers' opposition to efforts to provide choice within public education:

> Unsurprisingly, teachers' unions are often the most visible advocates questioning or objecting to charter expansion. In March 2013, American Federation of Teachers President Randi Weingarten was arrested in Philadelphia while protesting a district school-closing plan. Weingarten argued that the school closings would take money away from public schools while protecting charter schools, adding, "This was really a plan to eliminate public education." . . .
>
> Opponents of charter schools, including teachers' unions, emphasize the idea that charter school expansion is akin to the privatization of public education. Citing the dichotomy between those who view public education as an inherently public good and those who view the private sector as a better provider of services, charter school opponents emphasize the idea that for-profit pursuits in education may result in less accountability and transparency . . . Chicago Teachers' Union President Lewis has attacked the "venture capitalists" that she claims "use little black and brown children as stage props" in the fight to expand school choice options . . . Similarly, the National Education Association, the largest labor union in the United States, has stated that "privatization is a threat to public education and, more broadly, to our democracy itself." (Reckhow et al., 2013, referencing Resmovits, 2013; Ravitch, 2010; Boesenberg, 2003; Pearson 2013)

These sentiments are indicative of the official positions held by teacher organizations regarding efforts introduce choice within the American school system even though the charter-school movement is flourishing. Growth in the number of charter schools across the United States demonstrates why political support is so strong and how concerned parents are responding to the ongoing poor performance of the country's public-school system.

In Canada, opposition to charter schools remains firmly entrenched across the country, and the original effort by Alberta to introduce fifteen charter schools in the early 1990s remains the only official example.

Teachers' unions articulate their resistance to choice by opposing any amounts of public funding for independent schools, even though the *public purse saves money when parents exercise choice* and contribute significant personal funds. The public is easily fooled when unions chant, "No public dollars for private schooling." Their connotation is that a segment of the population is benefitting financially from attending private education. Many parents make financial sacrifices to enroll their children in private school.

Parents, pursuing private schooling, understand how they are double taxed because they pay taxes for public education as well as fees for their child's enrollment in private school. *They are challenging the misguided notion that all schools are equally effective*, and they are willing to pay extra dollars for acquiring educational services they believe are not available in their local school.

District administrators are *well aware that schools are not equally effective*, but their perceptions usually remain muted and confidential. Revelations concerning the substantial variances in quality of educational services could be a career-limiting move in a politically correct environment, where administrators' evaluations usually are influenced by their staff's perceptions. The education environment is too dominated by a culture of mutual back-scratching and back-slapping.

AMERICAN CHARTER-SCHOOL MOVEMENT

Charter schools represent another model of schooling that threatens to disrupt the virtual monopoly that now exists. They were instituted in the United States during reform efforts in the 1990s, and public support for this option has grown steadily since 1992. By 2000, approximately 2,000 charter schools were in place, increasing to 6,004 by 2012 and 2013, serving more than 2.2 million students in forty-two states and Washington, D.C. (National Alliance for Public Charter Schools Report). *Parents are voting with their feet.*

Public support for educational reform is not linked to support for the unions representing teachers, however. On January 13, 2016, the *Teachers Union Exposed* website published a post titled "Teachers Unions Oppose Education Reform," which described the control union leaders exercise on politicians:

> The control that union officials can maintain over local school boards borders on the ridiculous. Veteran education reporter Joe Williams wrote: "The United Teachers Los Angeles had such a tight grip on its school board in 2004 that

union leaders actually instructed them on important policies and made no attempt to hide their hand signals to school board members during meetings.

The post continued,

> Regardless of one's view of any particular method of improving America's struggling public schools (whether school choice, charter schools, or rewarding better teachers with better pay), the tactics and rhetoric that teachers' unions employ to block any meaningful reform is remarkable. Their motivation is simple: maintain the status quo—*and the flow of hundreds of millions of dollars in dues*. Meanwhile, union leaders' suggestions for reform are best summarized as "more money to hire more teachers," who are then likely to become dues-paying union members. (https://www.aftfacts.com)

Fitzgerald (2013) reported that money is the bottom line with teachers' labor leaders who worry about the public's right to choose: "Labor leaders say they want to organize charter schools because teachers are complaining about low pay and poor working conditions. Some observers, though, say the push toward unionization is to help unions boost their declining membership rolls." With only about 12 percent of charter-school staff unionized, both American teachers' unions have lost approximately 3 percent from 2011, according to the U.S. Department of Labor.

Critics within the education system attempt to stigmatize charter schools as raiders who cream more advantaged students from the traditional public schools. A report by Rebarber and Zgainer puts to *rest the myth that charter-school students are cherry-picked and less-disadvantaged than students in traditional public schools*:

> Charter students are somewhat more likely to qualify for free and reduced lunch due to being low-income (63 percent of charter students versus 48 percent of public-school students), to being African American (28 percent of charter students versus 16 percent of public-school students), or to being Hispanic (28 percent of charter students versus 23 percent of public-school students)....
>
> Many charter schools, especially those in urban environments, serve concentrated low-income and at-risk student populations. Sixty-one percent of charter schools serve student populations where more than 60 percent of students qualify for the free and reduced lunch program for low-income families.
>
> Similarly, 27 percent of charter schools serve populations with at least 60 percent of students categorized as at-risk. (Rebarber & Zgainer, 2014, pp. 8, 9)

The percentage of charter schools implementing *skill-based and performance-based* staff contracts has increased to 39 percent for the former and to 37 percent for the latter. Rebarber and Zgainer indicate that these increases are a positive trend that shows how, when given freedom, charter schools take hold of their own staffing authority and create a salary system based on skills and performance and reject the *fixed salary levels* that have been comfortably adhered to and influenced by teachers' unions to ensure uniformity across all public schools (Rebarber & Zgainer, 2014).

Many students are overwhelmed by the *pace of learning* required of them and can benefit from additional *time allotted for learning*. Today's curriculum is greatly expanded to assume emerging societal needs beyond basic education. Hence, considerably more learning and development is packed into today's schooling but without additional time provided. By 2014, 27 percent of charter schools provided an *extended school year*, and 48 percent increased the length of their school day.

Charter schools are accountable for their students' achievement. Their rules and structure are dependent on authorizing legislation, which differs across states. A charter school is authorized to function once it has received a charter: a statutorily defined performance contract detailing the school's mission, program, goals, students served, methods of assessment, and *ways to measure success*. The length of time for which charters are granted varies, but most are granted for three to five years, requiring a degree of success lest the school face the prospect of closure.

Accountability requires *consequences* when mandates are not achieved. As of March 2009, 12.5 percent of the over 5,000 charter schools founded in the United States had closed for reasons including academic, financial, and managerial problems and occasionally consolidation or district interference (Allen et al., 2009). This same level of accountability would produce dramatic educational reforms across America's public-school system.

The critical conclusion in discussing charter schools is that they are flourishing across the United States as parents make choices in schooling for their children. *Parents from all backgrounds are opting out of their restrictive public schools in order to take advantage of educational programing free from union control and more committed to serving their clients.*

CANADIAN CHARTER SCHOOLS

In Canada, only Alberta's government embraced charter schools, and Bennett (2010) describes educators' responses to the initiative:

> When the Alberta government of Ralph Klein authorized Canada's first charter schools, the core interests in Canadian education (school superintendents, education faculties, and teachers' unions) closed ranks and successfully fended off charter schools everywhere else. Instead of fairly evaluating charters as a means of broadening school choice, public-school authorities clicked into siege mentality mode, condemning the "privatizers" and casting aspersions on the motives of charter school advocates.

Bennett further indicates that this option for parents remains "a well-kept secret" to the rest of the country.

Notwithstanding the fact that charter schools have not been broadly established in Canada, an equivalent movement is evident. For example, in Alberta the Edmonton Public Schools (EPS) undertook dramatic action to promote school choice. In the late 1990s, EPS was heralded by researchers for implementing site-based decision-making and *opening boundaries for school choice*. Universal provincial testing was in its infancy, and reformers were *without access to data* on the implications for student achievement. Rather, their attention was drawn to the philosophical perspectives behind these initiatives.

PARENTAL INFLUENCE

When parents fulfill their responsibility to foster development in their child, their child's learning improves dramatically. The research on the extent of parental involvement on schooling reveals that parental commitment is greatest when children are in their early grades and that higher levels of socioeconomic indicators, including the parent's level of education, are significant determinants for parental support. *Overall, educators in the public-school system, in particular, lament the inadequacy of support from homes as students progress into higher grades.*

Motivating higher levels of parental involvement in their child's education is one of the purposes of this book. Providing parents with relevant information regarding a school's success is a necessary component for increasing their interest in the school system. This additional knowledge provides stimulus to seek and select the optimal learning environment for their child.

Choice is an essential trait in a democracy. Shoppers thrive when their opportunity to find bargains abounds. Governments are held to higher levels of accountability when voters have choices in the voting booth. Media is responsible for their reportage and held to account by their consumers. Vacation caterers offer higher-quality services to lure travelers who enjoy the freedom to travel almost anywhere. Competition provides the energy necessary for balancing cost and quality, and the public's freedom to choose simply increases satisfaction and commitment.

Wolfram (2018) explains how a different perspective dominates public education, saying, "We must make the transition from central planning to a market economy for the sake of our children." He continues,

> The government tells you what school you can attend, who is to be hired in the schools, and what is to be taught in the school.

> Nobel laureate Milton Friedman once compared our nation's education system to "an island of socialism in a free-market sea." Similarly, nearly 30 years ago, the then-president of the American Federation for Teachers Albert Shanker wrote, "It's time to admit that public education operates like a planned economy, a bureaucratic system in which everybody's role is spelled out in advance, and there are few incentives for innovation and productivity. It's no surprise that our school system doesn't improve: It more resembles the communist economy than our own market economy."

These insightful remarks provide impetus for policy makers to reduce government control of the education system, and this book's emphasis supports this charge by outlining why and how parental choice should be increased. School choice is not a viable option for most families, even though it does not represent a threat to the current monopoly. Opposition to choice is usually based on false fears and an aversion to competition and the stress created by comparisons. While all workers within the education system undoubtedly relish the benefits of choice in the market place, including schools within a free-market environment is troublesome because it adds pressure to perform and produce. In this scenario, a free market threatens survival.

Choice is also limited by school administrators wanting parents to accept the archaic belief that all schools can serve students equally. When parents vote with their feet, administrative issues must be resolved when particular schools are avoided and lack sufficient enrollment. Simply redrawing boundaries to capture additional students is no longer an option. Administrators are forced to examine programming and staffing issues to attract more clients to these schools.

MAGNET SCHOOLS

Educators' ongoing lamentations about a lack of parental involvement and support is no longer justified or appropriate. The same enthusiasm generated by a free-market approach to the distribution of goods and services could result in a new wave of commitment from parents. A model proposed in this chapter is to declare an *open-boundary system* within each school district and then to allow parents to pursue placement for their child in any school of their choosing. In other words, every school should be designated as a *magnet school*.

In a magnet-school concept, parents are no longer *assigned* a school for their child but are *drawn* to a school because of what the school is offering. Examining products for quality is a common goal within the marketplace. A similar perspective could dominate the education system if parents were able to review educational outcomes and then use the data to determine which school is best suited to their child's educational needs. Schools provide varying levels of instructional quality, and parents deserve knowing how effectively educators have been in serving their clients.

Equally important is *dispelling the myth that all schools can meet the needs of all students*. Schools, therefore, should attract their clientele by majoring in programs that appeal to the strengths and interests of specific students. Such programs may revolve around the arts, components of physical education and sport, languages, subject-area proficiencies leading to specific careers, special learning needs such as giftedness or learning difficulties, public speaking and presentations, technology and robotics, industry skills, social agencies, and so on. Schools could also choose to focus on a combination of programs from the foregoing list.

Naysayers to parental choice are likely to conjure up numerous "yeah-buts" for adopting an open-boundary system. After rejecting this concept, because it facilitates comparison and competition between schools, these cynics' main concern focuses on ensuring student access to their neighborhood school. Maintaining a prison mentality, where students are *confined* to a specific catchment or boundary, mitigates the benefits of a free-market system and is a matter requiring further analysis.

Alberta's Edmonton Public Schools, with a student population of almost 100,000, implemented school-based decision-making, where schools control all aspects of their budgets. This decentralization quickly morphed into control of a school's mission beyond core-education requirements. Parents living within a school's catchment retained first right-of-entry, leaving the remaining student spaces to parents from other parts of the school district. Our regional studies determined that only 48 percent of students attended their neighborhood's magnet school.

Many parents exercised an option to have their child attend a different school, basing their decision on issues such as the school's mission, academic record, special programming and services, and proximity to the parent's workplace, among other considerations. Earlier we outlined the academic success demonstrated by students in this school district who achieved *consistently improving test scores as they proceeded through the grades*.

Providing parents with the responsibility to select their child's school also motivates them to make certain that their choice is vindicated. Their dream of aligning their child's interest and talent with a specific school's mission inspires their own interest in the goals of the school and how well it is achieving. Edmonton Public School's success in achieving higher levels of academic success as students progress through the grades may have several contributing factors, and school choice must be included in the list.

Per-pupil funding is an issue when parents choose to enroll their children in different schools; however, the concern is readily resolved when all schools are within the same organizational structure or district. At the beginning of the school year, the funding allocated to each student follows that student to the appropriate school. Some school districts go a step further and make allowance for students changing schools during the term and apply a midterm adjustment. *The critical principle is that money follows a student to the selected school.*

COMPARING MAGNET, CHARTER, AND PRIVATE SCHOOLS

Magnet schools are somewhat similar to charter schools, with a few noteworthy differences. Charter schools are K–12 institutions, funded with taxpayer money *but managed privately*. They are semiautonomous, operating under a written contract with a state, district, or entity (referred to as an *authorizer* or *sponsor*). This contract—or charter—details how the school will be organized and managed, what students will be expected to achieve, and how success will be measured. Many charters are exempt from a variety of laws and regulations affecting other public schools if they continue to meet the terms of their charters.

These charter provisions incorporate higher levels of accountability, but their exemption from laws and regulations constraining other public schools has special appeal. While I was visiting one charter school along the California border with Mexico, which was also designated as America's top school, the principal provided significant insight into the school's lofty standing. In his opinion, a provision placing all staff on *one-year contracts* was the critical variable. Nonrenewal of a contract even jeopardized ongoing employment within the school district.

Magnet schools, on the other hand, are not semiautonomous but totally accountable to the local school board while operating within the jurisdiction's regulatory and contractual obligations. Rather than reporting to a semiautonomous board, they work with a parent advisory council (PAC). School administrators are obligated to *consult* with the PAC on matters such as the school mandate, education plan—including staff organization—the student-discipline policy, and other general matters. Another significant discussion activity involving the PAC follows the annual accumulation of results contained within the school's report card described earlier.

Sponsors, another critical component of charter schools, are not a requirement but a recommendation for magnet schools. Several partnerships can be identified that support the school's mission statement and provide opportunities for students to engage with the business community. Unlike sponsors, partnerships with magnet schools can be many and in competition with each other, and they can also change from year to year.

Private schools are a more dramatic approach to accommodating parent choice; however, they provide unique educational opportunities, such as religious instruction, for students. The private-school model frequently serves a community where many public schools are available. Registration into these private schools usually involves lining up on registration day, using a first-come-first-served model. Once a child is in the school, other family members receive preferential treatment.

A provision for ensuring that families are not separated should also be applied to magnet schools. In some respects, this commitment is antithetical to the magnet concept, because children in a family usually are different; however, parents may feel more comfortable knowing that family members are together. The choice to separate or be clannish is another element of parental choice.

In Canada, public funding for private schools is a contentious issue, with many educators voicing concern about their competition receiving financial support. Funding from provincial governments vary and is usually confined to a portion of the operating expenses. Private-school operators are responsible for generating funds for capital expenditures.

RESOLVING THE TRANSPORTATION LIMITATION

Regardless of the approach taken in schooling, choice is usually constrained by student-transportation issues. Indeed, cost and transportation arrangements are the main disqualifiers facing many parents interested in pursuing a more-appropriate educational experience for their child. Unfortunately, this transportation limitation *is most acutely experienced in single-parent and families of lower socioeconomic status*—the very groups of greatest concern to educators. There are exceptions within these classifications, but the generalization holds true.

Parental choice in school is a major force for reform in our education system and is made more viable when *transportation costs within the district are subsidized and even eliminated.* Free student transportation is almost as transformational as is choice in school, and these must go hand-in-hand. Yes, increased costs are incurred, because additional buses and drivers will be necessary; having said that, some school districts have adopted miniterminals within the district where many buses arrive and reroute students. The additional costs associated with free transportation to chosen schools is minimal compared with the waste evident in today's educational expenditures.

Some educators will view increased transportation costs as a deal-breaker because providing a democratic school system where parents can choose schools is, in their view, unnecessary. Saying that *a school is a school*, implying that all schools are equal, is as misguided as the old-fashioned belief that all teachers are equal. Our regional report cards for each school in the province reveals how dissimilar the achieved outcomes are among schools.

Easy access to school comparisons are too frequently not available. Perusing provincial and state websites related to school accountability is frustrating, because comparisons at the central level are not available and require Googling each school; or if results at the central level are online, comparisons require extensive research. These centralized sites are usually controlled by educators whose mind-set is opposed to comparisons, and then by politicians pandering to the educators for voting support.

The environment is drastically altered when a school system commits to open boundary with parents controlling which school their child will attend. Access to comparative information then becomes prominent, because parents are the clients searching for the most effective educational environments. Naturally some misinterpretations will occur, because parents, at this point, are viewed as unqualified "researchers," incapable of analyzing data appropriately.

Concern that democratizing the school system to this degree will require additional funding to accommodate the free-transportation component is legitimate but must be assessed in the context of how existing funds are wasted. North America's fixation for lowering class sizes was addressed when we debunked the belief that this was a *learning condition*, which it is not. Rather, it is a *working condition* cleverly positioned by teachers' unions as a necessary precondition for improving student achievement, which it has not.

Correcting this erroneous policy frequently employed by politicians pandering to voters is difficult, because the public is not privy to the overwhelming research demonstrating that lowering class size does not yield higher levels of student achievement. These failed attempts at reducing class sizes mean that there is now funding for the democratizing of the school system as proposed in this book and for the funding of numerous other initiatives, including increasing teacher salaries and providing bonuses for superior performance. Politicians in charge of the public purse are more fearful than fearless when taking on our nation's largest lobby group.

While the horse is out of the barn in the sense that it is now virtually impossible to claw back funding for already-reduced classes, nevertheless there is some likelihood that new funding formulas will be developed as innovation occurs elsewhere and that the reduction in class size will eventually be repealed. Educators represent approximately 3 percent of voters, and their political clout appeals to many politicians who have little regard for the prudent use of the people's money.

Another strategy for redeploying existing educational funds would be the abandonment of the long-standing practice of a twelve-month registration window in favor of one that lasts six months (Dueck, 2013). The current age spread in a grade is usually twelve months which, in the life of a six-year-old, is too large for grouping students in grade 1. While the physical spread in age may be only twelve months, the intellectual and maturity spread is considerably greater; indeed, the spread could be several years greater.

Our review of regional data identified a *failing-grade rate* of one in six by the end of grade 9, which was the unfortunate experience of students mostly born in the last four months of the registration window. The school system should review the efficacy of maintaining this twelve-month-registration window. It is ludicrous to blindly follow a policy that has been in place for centuries. Above all, we must acknowledge that children born in the second half of the registration window are not dumber but merely younger.

While some education authorities are increasing the age of school entry by a few months, they maintain the twelve-month window. Children compare their own success with that of their classmates even though this may be discouraged by their teachers. When a grade 1 student compares their success with someone who is 16 percent—or 364 days—older, self-esteem may be negatively impacted for years.

A six-month window significantly *reduces student failure* and enhances student achievement for academically talented students (Dueck, 2013). A conundrum facing educators is that these academically immature learners handicap the progress of their older classmates. *Teachers' moral imperative is to ensure that everyone achieves more than the minimum requirements, even at the expense of providing less services to the talented.* Hence the academic achievement of the older students declines as they proceed through their elementary schooling.

Initiating a policy for six-month-registration windows can achieve almost double-digit savings in educational expenditures, because fewer classes and classrooms are required, as are fewer teachers called upon for remedial teaching. In our research, the vast majority of the 16 percent of students spending an additional year in school to compensate for lack of academic success were born in the last four months of the registration window (Dueck, 2013). The savings from eliminating almost all remediation programs and teachers required to educate students for an additional year of schooling is much greater than costs associated with free transportation.

This chapter advocates for increased parental involvement in their child's education through the removal of school-boundary restrictions and encouraging choice. This free-enterprise approach encourages school innovation, because school staff endeavor to replace their cookie-cutter approaches and build programs around students. School-choice efforts currently in place frequently limit involvement, because transportation is an inhibitor; but this constraint can be overcome were a school system to implement free-busing arrangements.

Fulfilling a leadership role within a provincial jurisdiction required careful analysis of many opportunities for parental choice. We constantly advised the governments elected during this period to offer their unequivocal support, because we observed the benefits of magnet schools, home schooling, charter schools, and independent schools. The government's response was to increase financial support for those institutions, agreeing to the accountability required in the public-school system.

Chapter Thirteen

Using Student Report Cards for Schools

A six-year-old child is the most accountable worker in our culture. This shocking truth catches an astonishing reaction from every adult but is readily acknowledged when they understand that school is the student's workplace and report cards are a tool for accountability. Consider that each student receives a written formal evaluation of their work approximately fifty times before graduating twelve years later. The student's performance will be *rated* (symbols) and *ranked* (percentages/letter grades) in multiple subjects (reading, mathematics, etc.) and in multiple areas within each subject. Occasionally a "failing" assessment occurs, necessitating additional years in school.

This generalization about student accountability is particularly relevant in our school system. Impetus to ensure high educational standards came from the highest office in the United States. Consider the *New York Times* reportage of March 1, 2010, that "Obama Backs Rewarding Districts that Police Failing Schools" (Zeleny, 2010).

United States' President Obama, speaking to the U.S. Chamber of Commerce, made it very clear that "Our kids get only one chance at an education, and we need to get it right." Poor educational service for even one year can disadvantage students, placing them behind peers and below educational standards that reflect skills they will need for success later in life. "Getting it right" must be an annual concern (Zeleny, 2010).

We hold accountable what we value, and our current approach means that accountability in the public sector is undervalued. In education, the consequences are not merely an issue of pragmatism but of ethics. As Douglas Reeves (2004) eloquently put it, "As a fundamental moral principle, no child in any school will be more accountable than the adults in the system. Similarly, it is a moral principle of leadership that no teacher or staff member will be more accountable than the leaders in the system" (n.p.).

Webber et al. came to the same conclusion as Reeves. Their large-scale assessment regarding accountability in education concluded that "the teacher should be assessed more than the student" (Webber et al., 2009, n.p.). In other words, *what we do for children, we should do for the adults and organizations serving them*. This change in emphasis would be one of the most transformational approaches implemented within the school system.

We have already demonstrated the validity of using standardized testing as one measure for assessing school-district outcomes. Expanding the list to fully measure educational services is the purpose of this chapter; however, models were virtually nonexistent at the turn of the twenty-first century. Without a model as a working guideline, an assignment to develop a comprehensive design for the province's education system was a formidable task.

Three years of monthly negotiations with stakeholders produced an outcomes framework that provided the basis for identifying appropriate measures. Another year produced a system report card for evaluating each school and district. Stakeholder skepticism was a significant issue throughout, because a commercial model focused exclusively on *raw test scores*. In other words, the analysis ranked school performance without factoring in student socioeconomic status and whether the school's achievement was improving. Any system not scoring these two perspectives is invalid.

A commercial product published in newspapers provided *rankings* using *raw* scores, tallied on a ten-point scale. Our analysis of high schools in Alberta examined student achievement on provincial examinations leading to a graduation diploma. The 239 high schools were divided into rating categories from 1.0 to 10.0, and all of the schools in two large Alberta cities (Edmonton and Calgary) were rated and compared with the parents' average annual income for students within each school.

Raw scores for students from homes with an average annual income of less than $60,000 had an average ranking of 4.1 for Calgary and 4.3 for Edmonton. Homes with an average annual income greater than $110,000 scored an average ranking of 8.0 in both cities. Building a reporting system required common understanding of a better way to *rate and not merely rank* performance. Truly, students' raw scores could be predicted by knowing the price of their homes—a suitable proxy for income.

RAW VERSUS GAIN SCORES

Long-standing resistance to measuring the quality of school performance is passé, because measurement is now more sophisticated and meaningful. Recent refinements in performance measurement now make it possible to assess *gain scores* that measure *improvement* from baseline annually. Measuring *improvement* compares the most recent results with the past, such as attained by a three-year rolling average.

Alexander, Entwisle, and Olson (2001) studied student-achievement gains by socioeconomic level in reading and mathematics during the winter and summer seasons of a school year. Over a five-year period, student gains during each school year (winter) were virtually equal in both subjects; however, differences in gains during the summers, when students were away from school, favored students of higher socioeconomic status. All groups learned at the same rate while in school, but students of lower socioeconomic status either forgot more during the summer holidays because the home environment provided less stimulus or else had fewer opportunities (e.g., camps, travel, use of library, etc.) to engage in learning activities.

Miller also studied this issue of achievement gains by socioeconomic level and reported how all students benefit when school is in session but demonstrate different levels of achievement when the school is closed:

> During the school year, children in both affluent and lower-income communities benefit from what is known as the "faucet theory": Learning resources are turned on for all children during the school year. But in the summertime, the faucet is turned *off*. While all families want to provide the best for their children, there are significant differences between the resources middle-income families and communities can offer their children and what lower-income families and communities can offer. Even though low-income working families typically spend a higher portion of their income on child care than parents in more affluent families, even those with multiple low-wage jobs cannot cover the high tuition fees that are typical of many summer day and overnight camps. (Miller, 2007, pp. 7–8; emphasis in original)

Throughout the twentieth century, numerous studies have examined general learning loss among all students during the summer months. A meta-analysis of thirty-nine studies conducted since 1978 found that, over time when not actively in school school, all students score lower on standardized math tests at the end of the summer as compared to their performance on the same tests at the beginning of summer (Cooper, Nye, Charlton, Lindsay, & Greathouse, 1996).

These results are consistent with other researcher's findings that a family's socioeconomic status affects a child's achievement scores almost exclusively when school is closed. Heyns's (1978) landmark study of 2,978 6th and 7th graders in Atlanta public schools found that, while poor children and African American children came close to keeping up with middle-class children in cognitive growth when school was in session, they lagged far behind during the summer.

Researchers from the Ohio State University extended our understanding of the summer-learning gap by conducting a national study of 17,000 kindergarten and first-grade children from the Early Childhood Longitudinal Study. The authors confirmed earlier findings of an unequal starting point, showing that a standard deviation's advantage in socioeconomic status predicts a 1.77–month advantage in initial reading skill on the first day of kindergarten (Downey, von Hippel, & Broh, 2004). The authors also confirmed that the socioeconomic status–achievement gap continues to grow after schooling starts, with summer learning accounting for the vast majority of the difference.

The point is that raw scores on standardized tests favor students of higher socioeconomic status who are able to afford educational summertime activities, while students of lower socioeconomic status experience greater learning loss and less learning during the summer because they cannot afford as many of those same enriching activities. Standardized tests reflect standards, and disregarding students' raw scores on these tests is foolishness, because it unfairly shifts the goalposts measuring student achievement. *Measuring student achievement in a consistent manner while ensuring student anonymity rather than relying solely on a teacher's subjective classroom assessment is the most significant advancement in education's accountability movement.*

However, measuring only raw score is inadequate methodology when assessing the school system's performance. Yes, the public wants to know how well students are learning relative to *standards*, but it is equally important to know how well the school system is *improving* students' learning. Combining these two perspectives responds to and neutralizes criticisms that schools should be exempted from business-like practices such as accountability and its many components including measurement, transparency, competition, comparability, recognition, and consequences.

These studies underscore the need for incorporating *raw score* and *improvement data*. Failing to consider both variables provides an undeserved advantage to educators in schools where students benefit from their parent's higher economic status. Fullan (2005, p. 57) summarizes the predicament exceedingly well when he says, "Schools with traditionally high [raw] scores on achievement tests are no better off. These 'cruising schools' . . . get good results because the students are good in the first place. They show no particular evidence that the teachers are good in the way that [researchers] are talking about."

MULTIPLE CRITERIA

Just as students receive evaluations of their achievement for different subjects, school systems' evaluations should assess performance in multiple areas and, where necessary, from multiple sources—for example, from students, teachers, parents, and so on. The following serve as examples of aspects of school systems to be evaluated:

- *Safe and caring: Percentages of teachers, parents, and students who agree that students are safe at school are learning the importance of caring for others, are learning respect for others, and are treated fairly in school.* For example, teachers, parents, and students are asked whether students feel safe at school, students feel safe on the way to and from school, students treat each other well at school, teachers care about their students, and students are treated fairly by adults at school.
- *Program of studies: Percentages of teachers, parents, and students satisfied with the opportunity for students to receive a broad program of studies, including fine arts, career, technology, and health and physical education.* For example, teachers, parents, and students are asked about the variety of courses available to students at school and the opportunities students have at school to learn about music, drama, art, computers, health, and another language, as well as participate in physical education.
- *Education quality: Percentages of teachers, parents, and students satisfied with the overall quality of basic education.* For example, teachers, parents, and students are asked about the overall quality of education in the child's school, the quality of teaching in the child's school, whether what is being learned in the core subjects is useful to the students, whether students are learning what they need to know according to parents and teachers, whether the school work is interesting, whether the school work is challenging, and whether learning expectations at school are clear.
- *Satisfaction with program access: Percentages of teachers, parents, and students satisfied with the accessibility, effectiveness, and efficiency of programs and services for students in their community.* For example, teachers, parents, and students are asked about such services for student in schools as academic counseling, career counseling, library services, and supports for students with special needs.
- *Dropout rate: An assessment of the annual dropout rate of students aged 14 to 18.*
- *Three-year high school–completion rate: Percentages of students who completed high school within three years of entering grade 10.* The three- rather than four-year rate is chosen because it communicates a commitment to efficiency.
- *Student achievement: The scoring of tests for each group and subject assessed.*
- *Six-year postsecondary-transition rate: Percentages of students who have enrolled in a postsecondary program within six years of entering grade 10.*

- *Scholarship-eligibility rate: Percentages of grade 12 students who meet scholarship-eligibility criteria.*
- *Preparation for lifelong learning: Percentages of teachers and parents satisfied that high school graduates demonstrate the knowledge, skills, and attitudes necessary for lifelong learning.* For example, teachers and parents are asked whether high school students demonstrate the knowledge, skills, and attitudes necessary for learning throughout their lifetimes and whether students at the school are taught the knowledge, skills, and attitudes necessary for learning throughout their lifetimes.
- *Work preparation: Percentages of teachers and parents who agree that students are taught attitudes and behaviors that will make them successful at work when they finish school.* For example, teachers and parents are asked to indicate whether students in the school are taught attitudes and behaviors that will enable them to be successful at work when they leave school.
- *Citizenship: Percentages of teachers, parents, and students who are satisfied that students model the characteristics of active citizenship.* For example, teachers, parents, and students are asked whether students at the school help each other, respect each other, are encouraged at school to be involved in activities that help the community, are encouraged to try their best, and follow the rules.
- *Parental involvement: Percentages of teachers and parents satisfied with parental involvement in decisions about their child's education.* For example, teachers and parents are asked about the opportunity for parental involvement in decisions about their child's education, about the opportunity for parental involvement in decisions at their child's school, whether parental input into decisions at their child's school is considered, and whether parents are involved "a lot" or "some" with decisions about their child's education.
- *School improvement: Percentages of teachers, parents, and students indicating that their school and schools in their jurisdiction have improved or stayed the same over the last three years.* For example, teachers and parents are asked whether the quality of education at the school has improved, stayed the same, or declined in the past three years. Students are asked whether they are proud of their school and whether or not they would recommend the school to a friend.

Educators frequently criticize current accountability efforts for having too narrow a focus. Test results have been a convenient measure because they provide objective information easily conveyed to the public. Schooling is much more than test results in reading and mathematics. The extensive list above both addresses concerns regarding an overreliant emphasis on test results and assesses a broad array of factors in the school system that influence the education of our students.

SCHOOL-SYSTEM REPORT CARD

It is not necessary to invent new accountability criteria for schools and districts, because several are already available and used with students. For example:

- They are assessed on the basis of *ratings* rather than *rankings* where the focus is on both *achievement* relative to fixed standards and *improvement/decline* over time
- They are assessed using *multiple ratings* (as opposed to pass/fail) such as letter grades, scales of performance, and percentages or symbols
- They are assessed using *multiple measures*—like assessing knowledge retention in math, reading, and science, among other areas, as well as specific aspects within these areas of learning
- And they are held *personally accountable* for success determined annually at the end of the school year or course.

Recognizing that accountabilities should be implemented and aligned at both the individual and collective levels, building accountability and transparency within education's delivery units—schools, school districts, and states or provinces—is recommended. Fundamental principles underlying assessments at the unit level should include the following principles and actions:

- Reporting models should be *aligned* at the school, school-district, and state or provincial levels
- Measurement should incorporate both *quantitative* (e.g., test scores, graduation rates, etc.) and *qualitative* (e.g., student, parent, and staff satisfaction) data
- Evaluating results should utilize scales with *multiple ratings*
- Government has a *moral obligation to intervene* in cases of consistently poor performance
- Students only receive one chance at their education, and fairness requires they have an opportunity to *escape poor-performing schools*
- Transparency in reporting models is enhanced when the public is provided with *results* and easily discerned *evaluations* of performance (e.g., letter grades, color codes, etc.)
- And accountability requires *consequences*, and both positive and negative consequences must be outlined and applied.

In 2015 the U.S. Congress initiated a bold attempt to incorporate meaningful accountability and transparency within the U.S. public-school system. Even though education is a state responsibility, Congress's action was deemed appropriate because Congress contributes funding for education (approximately 10 percent of all public-school funding in a year) and because to do so aligns with other federal-government education initiatives launched by President George W. Bush (No Child Left Behind) and President Barack Obama (Race to the Top).

The following points should be part of a state or provincial assessment system:

- Performance should be assessed and reported annually
- System testing requires a balanced emphasis on the four core subjects and therefore should be in language arts, mathematics, science, and social studies
- System tests in language arts and mathematics should be written each year by students in grades 3 through 8 and at least once in high school—preferably grade 12—while testing in science and social studies should occur at least once in grades 3–5, 6–8, and one grade in high school—preferably grade 12
- Student success on system tests should be assessed using a minimum of two levels of achievement—basic and advanced—while a second option would score using three levels—basic, proficient, and advanced
- Reporting on student academic success should be based on two groupings of students:

  - *All students* using *cohort* reporting, so that every level of the school system shares responsibility for pursuing all students' participation, where the motivation within this cohort approach is to advance as many students as possible toward higher educational standards
  - And *selected students* based on students writing the test for (1) economically disadvantaged students, (2) students from major racial and ethnic groups, (3) children with disabilities, and (4) English learner

- As outlined in chapter 6, an additional academic indicator for grades 1 through 8 should be based on grade level of achievement (GLA) at the conclusion of the school year for all students in language arts and mathematics, specifying whether student achievement has been at grade level, below grade level, or above grade level. Note that acquiring the teacher's assessment provides balance with system testing and is safeguarded from erroneous grade inflation by having each teacher's assessment recorded for follow-up discussion between teachers and principal in subsequent years.

- A secondary-school measure should be defined as the percentage of students who graduate from secondary school within four years
- An additional secondary-school measure should be based on school climate and safety
- Reporting results should be based on both achievement relative to fixed standards as well as improvement over time
- Results are reported publicly at the school, school-district, and state levels and should be broken down to the classroom level whenever possible for each school principal's use with their teachers
- Student-, parent-, and staff-satisfaction levels with various services and support should be ascertained
- And attendance levels for staff and students should be recorded.

Evaluating performance, a task frequently avoided, is the final aspect in constructing report cards for schools, districts, and states or provinces. Merely presenting data is insufficient for understanding how well a system is performing, and in my experience publicly negotiating the evaluation standards necessitated input from stakeholders as well as thousands of citizens across the region. In the end, we agreed to use a five-point evaluation scale for both *raw* and *improvement* scores (Dueck, 2018).

Report cards are enhanced when their construction considers the power of a reader's eye gate. A verbal scale for each measure—for example, assessing performance as significantly improved, improved, satisfactory, declined, significantly declined—provides readers with information similar to scales used with students' report cards. But applying colors to scale performance—like top-quality performance denoted by blue, scaling to green, yellow, orange, and finally red, which denotes the lowest-quality performance—simplifies understanding, because peoples' eyes focus more quickly on colors than words.

Building an evaluation program incorporating similar principles used in student reporting is a transformative step in maintaining educational accountability. When in place, this reporting provides the basis for assessing leadership and attaching positive and negative consequences to performance (Dueck, 2018). Indeed, these consequences are applicable not only for education administrators but also for state politicians who manage the education system for taxpayers, the school system's clients.

Using report cards for assessing the quality of educational services is controversial with providers, even though they use report cards with their students. During the time period when Alberta developed its publicly acclaimed Accountability Pillar—a report card for every school, district, and provincial system—teachers opposed the initiative. A survey of the province's parents and teachers found that 85 percent of parents agreed that

"There should be an annual report card for schools just as for students." Only 47 percent of teachers, however, agreed.

Inherent resistance by service providers to accountability is understandable. While educators deem it necessary to hold students accountable for their learning, educators are not as sanguine about being held accountable themselves. Their service to our society is of such importance, however, that school-system leadership must boldly act to establish an accountability program incorporating consequences, both positive and negative.

Conclusion

Today's educational system is undergoing massive change, transitioning from minimal accountability to efforts more in keeping with the types of accountability found in free enterprise. This change has not been coordinated in a logical manner but, rather, is proceeding haphazardly, with leaders of the changes committed to shifting power from educators to parents. This broken-front approach is necessary, because workers in education can vote even though their immediate clients, our children, cannot. Simply stated, our politicians choose to disregard what is in students' best interests, requiring contentious efforts from individual leaders to blaze the trail for reform.

This book outlines efforts to change our educational system, from providing management services to leadership functions in the educational enterprise. For school principals, leadership involves meeting the needs of the school's immediate constituents—students, teachers, and parents. Encouraging parent participation in the school and holding staff and students to high expectations provide a recipe for success.

Advancing change into senior levels of leadership in school districts and provincial positions requires fortitude, supported with powerful research. Teacher unions frequently present the most significant obstacles to reform, because their members experience increased pressure to improve performance emanating from accountability programs. Accountability is the most effective investment! School and district report cards, using standardized test results as well as other measures, both quantitative and qualitative, introduce comparability and competition within the provincial and state-level education system.

Accountability provides parents with information necessary for choosing schools most aligned with their values and needs. This power to choose is an important attribute leading to transformational change within education, threatened only by politicians' acquiescing to educators who clamor for a return to an assessment system without the consistent standards possible only through standardized testing and accompanied by anonymous marking. The change leader's responsibility is ensuring that our students' only chance for a quality education is a reality.

References

Alexander, K. L., Entwisle, D. R., & Olson, L. S. (2001). Schools, achievement, and inequality: A seasonal perspective. *Educational Evaluation and Policy Analysis, 23*(2), 171–91.

Allen, C., Chen, Q., Willson, V., & Hughes, J. N. (2009). Quality of design moderates effects of grade retention on achievement: A meta-analytic, multi-level analysis. *Educational Evaluation and Policy Analysis, 31*, 480–99.

Allen. (2009). National Alliance for Public Charter Schools.

Anderson, J. (2013, March 30). Curious grade for teachers: Nearly all pass." *New York Times*. Retrieved from https://www.nytimes.com/2013/03/31/education/curious-grade-for-teachers-nearly-all-pass.html

Babcock, P. (2010). Real costs of nominal grade inflation? New evidence from student course evaluations." *Economic Inquiry, 48*(4), 983–96. https://doi.org/10.1111/j.1465-7295.2009.00245.x

Baker, A. (2014, February 4). A call to ignore exam results when evaluating educators. *New York Times*. Retrieved from https://www.nytimes.com/2014/02/05/nyregion/a-call-to-ignore-exam-results-when-evaluating-educators.html.

Bennett, P. W. (2010, April 10). A well-kept secret: Whatever happened to Canada's charter schools? *Our Kids*. Retrieved from https://www.gopetition.com/petitions/support-charter-schools-in-ontario.html

Bevan, Y., Brighouse, T., Mills, G., Rose, J., & Smith, M. (2009). *Report of the expert group on assessment*. London: Crown Copyright. Retrieved from https://www.education.gov.uk/publications/eOrderingDownload/Expert-Group-Report.pdf

Bishop, J. H. (1997). *Do curriculum-based external exit exam systems enhance student achievement?* Ithaca, NY: Center for Advanced Human Resource Studies, Cornell University, ILR School.

———. (2002, April). What should be the federal role in supporting and shaping development of state accountability systems for secondary school achievement? (Paper prepared for the Office of Vocational and Adult Education, US Department of Education. Retrieved from https://webcache.googleusercontent.com/search?q=cache:M0uVk2yNXbIJ:https://www2.ed.gov/about/offices/list/ovae/pi/hs/bishop.doc+&cd=2&hl=en&ct=clnk&gl=us&client=safari

Black, P., Harris, C., Lee, C., Marshall, B., & William, D. (2003). *Assessment for learning: Putting it into practice*. New York: Open University Press.

Boesenberg, E. (2003). Privatizing public schools: Education in the marketplace. *Workplace: A Journal for Academic Labor, 5*(2). Retrieved from http://louisville.edu/journal/workplace/issue5p2/boesenberg.html

Bushway, A., & Nash, W. R. (1977). School cheating behaviour. *Review of Educational Research, 47*(4), 623–32.

Chilcott, L. (Producer) & Guggenheim, D. (Director). (2010). *Waiting for "Superman"* [Motion picture]. United States of America: Walden Media and Paramount Vantage.

Clark, J. (2017, April 12). Where corporal punishment is still used in schools, its roots run deep. NPR. Retrieved from https://www.npr.org/sections/ed/2017/04/12/521944429/where-corporal-punishment-is-still-used-its-roots-go-deep

Cooper, H., Nye, B., Charlton, K., Lindsay, J., & Greathouse, S. (1996). The effects of summer vacation on achievement test scores: A narrative and meta-analytic review. *Review of Educational Research, 66*(3), 227–68.

Côté, J. (2009). Identity formation and self-development in adolescence. In R. M. Lerner & L. Steinberg (Eds.), *Handbook of adolescent psychology* (vol. 1, *Individual bases of adolescent development*) (pp. 266–304). Hoboken, NJ: John Wiley & Sons, Inc.

Côté, J., & Anton, A. (2007). *The ivory tower blues: A university in crisis.* Toronto: University of Toronto Press.

Craft, H. (2014, September 24). The myth of teacher objectivity in student assessment. *Controversial issues in public education.* Retrieved from https://teachingdoneright.blogspot.com/2014/09/the-myth-of-teacher-objectivity-in.html

Cunningham, W. G., & Owens, R. C. (1976, October). Social promotion: Problem or solution? *NASSP Bulletin, 60*(402), 25–29.

Davis, S. F., Drinan, P. F., & Gallant, T. B. (2009). *Cheating in school.* Chichester, UK: Wiley-Blackwell.

Decoo, W. (2002). *Crisis on campus: Confronting academic misconduct.* Cambridge, MA: MIT Press.

Downey, D. B., von Hippel, P. T., & Broh, B. (2004). Are schools the great equalizer? Cognitive inequality during the summer months and the school year. *American Sociological Review, 69*(5), 613–35.

Dueck, J. (2013). *Being fair with kids: The effects of poor leadership in rule making.* Lanham, MD: Rowman & Littlefield Publishing Group.

———. (2014). *Education's flashpoints: Upside-down or set up to fail.* Lanham, MD: Rowman & Littlefield.

———. (2017). *Gender fairness in today's school: A breach of trust for male students.* Lanham, MD: Rowman & Littlefield.

———. (2018). *Accountable schools: Succeeding today in the competitive marketplace.* Lanham, MD: Rowman & Littlefield.

Fitzgerald, S. (2013, April 16). Teachers unions targeting charter schools. *Newsmax.* Retrieved from https://www.newsmax.com/US/teachers-union-charter-schools/2013/04/16/id/499683/

Frenette, M., & Zeman, K. (2007, September). *Why are most university students women? Evidence based on academic performance, study habits and parental influence.* Ottawa: Statistics Canada. Retrieved from https://www.researchgate.net/publication/23546183_Why_Are_Most_University_Students_Women_Evidence_Based_on_Academic_Performance_Study_Habits_and_Parental_Influences

Fullan, M. (2005). *Leadership & sustainability: System thinkers in action.* Thousand Oaks, CA: Sage Publications.

———. (2009). Positive pressure. In A. Hargreaves, A. Lieberman, M. Fullan, D. Hopkins, & C. Stone-Johnson (Eds.), *Second international handbook of educational change* (Vol. 23), Springer International Handbooks of Education (pp. 119–30). Dordrecht, Heidelberg, London, & New York: Springer. Retrieved from https://www.essr.net/~jafundo/mestrado_material_itgjkhnld/Material%20Prof%20Ilidiaichael%20Fullan,%20David%20Hopkins%20Second%20International%20Handbook%20of%20Educational%20Change,%20Part%20I%20Springer%20International%20Handbooks%20of%20Education%2032%20%202020 10.pdf

Gardner, H. (1983). *Frames of mind: The theories of multiple intelligences.* New York: Basic Books.

Greene, J. P., & Winters, M. A. (2011, March 3). Test-based promotion proves its mettle. *Nevada News and Views*. Retrieved from http://nevadanewsandviews.com/test-based-promotion-proves-its-mettle/

Gurian, M., & Stevens, K. (2006, October). Learning and gender. *American School Board Journal*. Retrieved from http://whitehouseboysmen.org/learning-and-gender

Guthrie, J. W. (Ed.). (2003). *The encyclopedia of education* (2nd ed.). New York: Thomson Gale.

Harlen, W. (2004, December). *A systematic review of the evidence of the impact on students, teachers and the curriculum of the process of using assessment by teachers for summative purposes: Review conducted by the Assessment and Learning Research Synthesis Group*. London: EPPI-Centre. Retrieved from https://eppi.ioe.ac.uk/cms/Portals/0/PDF%20reviews%20and%20summaries/ass_rv4.pdf?ver=2006-03-02-124724-997

———. (2005). Trusting teachers' judgment: Research evidence of the reliability and validity of teachers' assessment used for summative purposes. *Research Papers in Education, 20*(3): 245–70.

Hawke, P. (2006). Report card on Florida schools policy to end social promotion. *Schools K–12*. Retrieved from https://www.schoolsk-12.com/parents/Report-Card-on-Florida-Schools-Policy-to-End-Social-Promotion.html

Heyns, B. (1978). *Summer learning and the effects of schooling*. New York: Academic Press.

Ho, L. (2012). School isn't about education any more; it's about getting good grades and that increases the pressure. *Vancouver Sun*, March 27, 2012.

Josephson Institute of Ethics. (2002). *2002 Report Card on the Ethics of American Youth*. Retrieved from

Karweit, N. L. (1999). *Grade retention: Prevalence, timing, and effects*. Report no. 33. Baltimore: John Hopkins University, CRESPAR.

Kirby, S., Naftel, S., McCombs, J., Gershwin, D., and Creg, A. (2009). Performance of 5th Graders in New York City and Overall Performance Trends in New York State. *Ending Social Promotion Without Leaving Children Behind: The Case of New York City*, www.rand.org.

Koedel, C. (2011, August 22). Grade inflation for education majors and low standards for teachers. *American Enterprise Institute* (7). Retrieved from http://www.aei.org/publication/grade-inflation-for-education-majors-and-low-standards-for-teachers/

Laurie, L. "Grade inflation sets up students to fail: Study." Halifax, Nova Scotia: *Atlantic Institute for Marketing*, 2007.

Lorence, J. (2006). Retention and academic achievement research revisited from a United States perspective. *International Education Journal, 7*(5), 731–77. Retrieved from https://files.eric.ed.gov/fulltext/EJ854336.pdf

Mahoney, Jill. (2007, June 9). Why children no longer flunk in school. *The Globe and Mail*. Updated April 28, 2018. Retrieved from https://www.theglobeandmail.com/news/national/why-children-no-longer-flunk-in-school/article687488/

McCabe, D. L., Treviño, L. K., & Butterfield, K. D. (2001, July). Cheating in academic institutions: A decade of research. *Ethics & Behavior, 11*(3), 219–32. Retrieved from https://www.researchgate.net/publication/228603457_Cheating_in_Academic_Institutions_A_Decade_of_Research

McClure, M. (2011, November 29). National standards sought for exams. *Calgary Herald*.

McCombs, J. S., Kirby, S. N., & Mariano, L. T. (Eds.). (2009). *Ending social promotion without leaving children behind: The case of New York City*. Santa Monica, CA: RAND Corporation. Retrieved from https://www.rand.org/content/dam/rand/pubs/monographs/2009/RAND_MG894.pdf

McGuire, J. (2016, November 23). What states allow schools to use corporal punishment? Far too many. *Romper*. Retrieved from https://www.romper.com/p/what-states-allow-schools-to-use-corporal-punishment-far-too-many-23409

Mellon, E. (2010, January 14). HISD moves ahead on policy to fire teachers over test scores. *Houston Chronicle*. Retrieved from https://www.chron.com/news/houston-texas/article/HISD-moves-ahead-on-policy-to-fire-teachers-over-1705328.php

Miller, B. M. (2007, June). *The learning season: The untapped power of summer to advance student achievement; executive summary*. Quincy, MA: Nellie Mae Education Foundation. Retrieved from https://www.nmefoundation.org/getmedia/17ce8652-b952-4706-851b-bf8458cec62e/Learning-Season-ES?ext=.pdf

Millington, C. (2011, November 28). Proof there's grade 12 marks inflation. *Canada University Admit*. Retrieved from http://canadauniversityadmit.blogspot.com/2011/11/high-school-grade-inflation.html

Molnar, M. (2013). Graduation Rates, Dropout "Recovery" Focus of Education Week Report. *Education Week*, June 7, 2013.

National Association of School Psychologists. (2011). Grade retention and social promotion (White paper). Bethesda, MD: Author. Retrieved from https://www.nasponline.org/x32088.xml

National Education Association. (2012, January 6). NEA president says misuse of standardized tests must stop. Retrieved from http://www.nea.org/archive/50296.htm

Newberger, E. H. (1999). *The men they will become: The nature and nurture of the male character*. Reading, MA: Perseus Publishing.

Organisation for Economic Co-operation and Development. (2012.) *Grade expectations: How marks and education policies shape students' ambitions*. Paris: PISA, OECD Publishing.

Pearson, R. (2013, June 19). CTU's Lewis rips Emanuel's "elite" advisers. *Chicago Tribune*. Retrieved from http://www.chicagotribune.com/news/politics/clout/chi-ctus-lewis-rips-emanuels-elite-advisers-20130618,0,1768021.story

Peter D. Hart Research Associates. (1995). *Valuable views: A public opinion research report on the views of AFT teachers on professional issues*. Washington, DC: American Federation of Teachers.

Phelps, R. P. (2003). *Kill the messenger: The war on standardized testing*. New Brunswick, NJ: Transaction.

———. (2008, June 3). The role and importance of standardized testing in the world of teaching and training. Paper presented at the 15th Congress of the World Association for Educational Research, Cadi Ayyad University, Marrakesh, Morocco. Retrieved from https://nonpartisaneducation.org/Review/Essays/v4n3.pdf

Public Agenda. (2001, February 21). Social promotion is declining steadily in schools. (Press release.) Retrieved from https://www.publicagenda.org/press-releases/social-promotion-declining-steadily-us-schools

Ravitch, D. (2010, November 11). The myth of charter schools. *The New York Review of Books*. Retrieved from http://www.nybooks.com/articles/archives/2010/nov/11/myth-charter-schools/

Rebarber, T., & Zgainer, A. C. (Eds.). (2014). *Survey of America's charter schools, 2014: The essential guide to charter school operations*. Washington, DC: The Center for Education Reform. Retrieved from https://issuu.com/centerforedreform/docs/2014charterschoolsurveyfinal_7864baf3fe08cd

Reckhow, S., Grossman, M., & Chung Evans, B. (2013). *Policy cues and ideology in attitudes toward charter schools*. East Lansing, MI: Michigan State University, Education Policy Center.

Reeves, D. B. (2004). *Accountability for learning: How teachers and school leaders can take charge*. Alexandria, VA: Association for Supervision and Curriculum Development.

Resmovits, J. (2013, March 7). Randi Weingerten arrested for protesting Philadelphia school closure hearings (updated). *Huffington Post*. Retrieved from https://www.huffpost.com/entry/randi-weingarten-arrested_n_2832306

Ryan, J. J. C. H. (1998, December). Student plagiarism in an online world. *ASEE Prism Magazine*. Retrieved from http://www.prism-magazine.org/december/html/student_plagiarism_in_an_onlin.htm

Sands, A. (2013, February 22). Education minister aims to kickstart talks with new offer to Alberta teachers. *Edmonton Journal*.

———. (2014, May 23). Computers top teachers in marking, study says. *Calgary Herald*. Text retrieved from http://joe-bower.blogspot.com/2014/05/computers-dramatically-more-reliable.html

Scantlebury, K. (2009). Gender bias in teaching. In E. Anderman (Ed.). *Psychology of classroom learning: An encyclopedia* (pp. 221–24). Detroit: Macmillan Reference USA.

Steffenhagen, J. (2012, March 22). UCB acknowledges tougher grading in Alberta. *Vancouver Sun*. Retrieved from https://vancouversun.com/news/staff-blogs/ubc-acknowledges-tougher-grading-in-alberta

The Telegraph. (2009, August 20.) A-level results: Grade inflation is just a cruel confidence trick. Retrieved from http://www.telegraph.co.uk/comment/6063012/A-level-results-grade-inflation-is-just-a-cruel-confidence-trick.html

Thomas, M. D., & Bainbridge, W. L. (1997, January). Grade inflation: The current fraud. *Effective School Research*.

Thompson, C. L., & Cunningham, E. K. (2000, December). Retention and social promotion: Research and implications for policy. *ERIC Digest* (161). ERIC Identifier: ED449241. Retrieved from https://www.ericdigests.org/2001-3/policy.htm

University of Alberta. (2011, June). *Summary of statistics, 2010–2011*. Retrieved from http://www.registrarsoffice.ualberta.ca/General-Information/~/media/registrar/sosfiles/2010-2011/Summary_of_Statistics_2010_11_Book.pdf

U.S. Department of Education, National Center for Education Statistics. (2006). The Condition of Education 2006 (NCES 2006-071). Washington, DC: U.S. Government Printing Office.

Voyer, D. (2014, April 29). Girls make higher grades than boys in all school subjects, analysis finds. *American Psychological Association*. Retrieved from https://www.apa.org/news/press/releases/2014/04/girls-grades

Wall, C. N. (2003). The skewing of the bell curve: A study of grade inflation in Oklahoma high schools. Biosurvey.ou.edu/oas/03/paper/wall.htm

Webber, C. F., Aitken, N., Lupart, J., & Scott, S. (2009). The Alberta student assessment study: Final report. Edmonton, AB: Alberta Education. Retrieved from https://archive.org/details/albertastudentas00webb

Wolfram, G. (2018, January 5). Make public education a market economy—not a socialist one. *Education Week*. Retrieved from https://www.edweek.org/ew/articles/2018/01/08/make-public-education-a-market-economy--not-a.html

Woods, M. (2008, September 19). Making the grade. *The Queen's Journal*. Retrieved from https://www.queensjournal.ca/story/2008-09-19/features/making-the-grade/

Xiang, Y., Dahlin, M., Cronin, J., Theaker, R., & Durant, S. (2011, September 20). Do high flyers maintain their altitude? Performance trends of top students. Thomas B. Fordham Institute. Retrieved from https://files.eric.ed.gov/fulltext/ED524344.pdf

Zeleny, J. (2010, March 1). Obama backs rewarding districts that police failing schools. *New York Times*. Retrieved from https://www.nytimes.com/2010/03/02/us/02obama.html

www.ingramcontent.com/pod-product-compliance
Lightning Source LLC
Chambersburg PA
CBHW020740230426
43665CB00009B/503